RAF

COASTAL COMMAND
IN ACTION
1939–1945

RAF

COASTAL COMMAND
IN ACTION

1939–1945

ROY CONYERS NESBIT

Assisted by Oliver Hoare

SUTTON PUBLISHING LIMITED

IN ASSOCIATION WITH THE PUBLIC RECORD OFFICE

First published in 1997 by
Sutton Publishing Limited · Phoenix Mill
Thrupp · Stroud · Gloucestershire · GL5 2BU

British Library Cataloguing in Publication Data
A catalogue record for this book is available from the British Library

ISBN 0 7509 1565 X

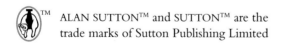

ALAN SUTTON™ and SUTTON™ are the
trade marks of Sutton Publishing Limited

Typeset in 11/15pt Baskerville
Typesetting and origination by
Sutton Publishing Limited
Printed in Great Britain by
Butler & Tanner, Frome, Somerset.

CONTENTS

INTRODUCTION

The photographs in this book represent the work of RAF Coastal Command during the Second World War. The majority were taken in action against the enemy, with F24 cameras either in a fixed position or hand-held by a crew member such as the wireless operator. Others were taken by G45 gun cameras facing forward and operated when the pilot pressed the firing button. Although the results can be very dramatic, they seldom show the full circumstances of the action. Most attacks by Coastal Command took place in daylight at extreme low level against intense light flak, such as 7.92-mm machine-gun bullets or 20-mm explosive cannon shells. Both attacker and defender fired at point-blank range but in daylight the tracer used in their bullets or shells does not show up in the films, although sometimes splashes in the sea can be seen. Several of the photographs are rather blurred. These were taken by a crew member while the pilot was jinking the aircraft to avoid flak, and are included for historical interest.

It is not generally recognized that Coastal Command's anti-shipping operations could be extremely dangerous

and that in fact the losses suffered by some of its squadrons were far heavier than those in any other Command. Indeed, at one time the rate of surviving a single tour in a torpedo-bomber squadron was officially assessed as no more than 17.5 per cent.

These photographs are scattered in many documents such as the Operations Record Books of squadrons and stations, or in intelligence reports. Although copies of some photographs can be found in other national collections, a particular merit of the originals in the Public Record Office is that many of those taken from the air have details printed along their edges giving information such as squadron number, date, time, place, height of aircraft and name of target. These details have been cropped from the prints in this book, but obviously the originals provided important leads for further research.

The author is acutely aware that the photographs in this book cover only some of Coastal Command's activities in the Second World War and that there were. many extremely gallant actions during which photographs could not be taken. Moreover, only a tiny proportion of those taken have survived for posterity. Some squadron and station adjutants took the trouble to affix photographs to their records while others did not. For this reason, the selection here tends to be unbalanced, with some squadrons not represented at all. One important section has been deliberately omitted, apart from a couple of examples. This is the work of the specialized photo-reconnaissance units and squadrons, which came under the control of Coastal Command for the majority of the war but were mostly devoted to the attacks made by Bomber Command, the US Eighth Air Force and the 2nd Tactical Air Force. Such photographs are best contained in a separate book. However, for the benefit of readers, an appendix listing the sources of many other Coastal Command photographs is included.

The captions underneath the photographs are based partly on the documents in which they were located, supplemented by a considerable amount of research in other relevant documents in the PRO and elsewhere. Readers who wish to carry out similar research are recommended to purchase a copy of PRO Readers' Guide No. 8 *RAF Records in the PRO* by Simon Fowler, Peter Elliott, Roy Conyers Nesbit and Christina Goulter (PRO Publications 1994), available from the PRO shop at the Public Record Office, Ruskin Avenue, Kew, Richmond, Surrey TW9 4DU. This guide also includes an appendix listing some other sources of RAF photographs within Great Britain.

Copies of any photographs housed in the PRO and required for commercial reproduction or private use can be obtained from the PRO Image Library, telephone 0181-392-5255. Prices will be given on request.

ACKNOWLEDGEMENTS

My thanks are due to colleagues at the Public Record Office: Julia Wigg for her help in producing the book; Oliver Hoare for his considerable assistance in finding and researching the photographs; and Brian Carter for his expert work in copying the photographs housed in numerous documents.

Much additional help with research for the captions was provided by Rick Chapman in Germany, Robert M. Coppock of Naval Staff Duties at the MoD, Air Cdre Jeaffreson H. Greswell RAF (Ret'd), Clive Richards of the Air Historical Branch (RAF) at the MoD, Richard S. Robinson, Juan Carlos Salgado in Spain, Ernest Schofield, Halvor Sperbund in Norway, and Gerrit J. Zwanenburg in the Netherlands.

Finally, I am extremely grateful to those who painstakingly checked the draft of the book and made indispensable comments for improvement. They are Dudley Cowderoy, Jack Eggleston and Roger Hayward. Any errors which remain after this expertise are my own responsibility.

Outrageous Fortune
September 1939 – June 1940

At the outbreak of the Second World War, Coastal Command consisted of only 183 aircraft. Of these, 135 were Avro Ansons, a reliable aircraft but one with inadequate armament, low bomb-carrying capacity and insufficient range. Only nine were Lockheed Hudsons, chosen as the main replacement for the Ansons. There were sixteen Short Sunderlands, but others were in production to replace the fifteen obsolescent Saro London or Supermarine Stranraer flying boats still in service. However, the anti-submarine bombs which the aircraft carried were almost useless, even if they scored a direct hit, and depth charges which could be dropped from the air were not yet designed. The anti-shipping strike force consisted merely of twelve Vickers Vildebeests, an obsolete torpedo-carrying biplane, although Bristol Beauforts were being built to replace these.

Such an inadequate force was not quite so ridiculous as it may seem in retrospect. Germany's North Sea coastline was short and the main enemy threat was believed to come from surface raiders and U-boats. Defence against the Kriegsmarine was considered to be the province of the powerful Royal Navy, backed by its Fleet Air Arm. The duties of Coastal Command were perceived as reconnaissance, convoy escort and submarine spotting, with an occasional foray against enemy warships. Although more advanced aircraft were in production for the RAF, the Command was given a far lower priority in Britain's belated rearmament programme than its sister Commands. Of course, it would have been a most unusual and prescient military analyst who could have foreseen the catastrophes which would befall the French and British forces in the first ten months of the war and the enormous extra burdens which would be heaped on Coastal Command.

The main strength of the Command lay in its personnel rather than its equipment. The pilots were highly skilled, trained in long-distance flying and navigation over the sea, as well as in many matters relating to general reconnaissance. Some of them were experienced in flying in the RAF's overseas Commands, over vast stretches of seas and oceans. They considered themselves an élite. Those of junior rank who survived the early months of the war were rapidly promoted to command flights, squadrons and even stations. They formed the basis for a Command which steadily overcame its problems and became an irresistible force which made a major contribution to the ultimate victory.

The appellation 'Phoney War' which characterized many of the military activities of those early months did not apply to Coastal Command. Its squadrons were at full stretch from the outset, primarily engaged on convoy escort and air reconnaissance. Combats with enemy aircraft were not infrequent, especially over the dangerous waters near the south of Norway, and losses mounted. Gibraltar came under the Command from the first week of the war. However, only one U-boat was sunk by the Command in the period covered by this first chapter, and that was shared with HM ships. Meanwhile the aircrews watched as U-boats and mines took their toll of British merchant vessels. Attacks against enemy merchant vessels were forbidden until the Germans invaded Denmark and Norway in April 1940, unless the aircrews were sure that they were surface raiders or connected with them. Only one enemy warship was sunk by the Command in this period, a minesweeper off Norway. The Command took little part in combating the successes of the Wehrmacht in the West, apart from providing some support to British naval units. When France collapsed in June 1940, it faced a situation that was even more desperate than that of the other RAF Commands.

The Lockheed Hudson began to enter service with Coastal Command in May 1939, gradually replacing the Avro Anson as the main land-based reconnaissance aircraft. Armed with up to seven machine guns, it had the range to reach ports in south-west Norway and thus close the gap in the North Sea. Although not ideal as an anti-shipping strike aircraft, it gave excellent front-line service, including an important role in air-sea rescue. Hudsons were manufactured in the USA and this example, serial T9465 of 269 Squadron, was made by employees of Lockheed-Vega in their spare time from material given by their company and donated to the RAF. It was photographed over Iceland against the background of a glacier and lava slopes.
Ref: AIR 15/470

On 21 September 1939, 224 Squadron despatched two Hudson Is from Thornaby in Yorkshire to photograph German naval vessels in the German island of Heligoland. They were serial N7219 flown by Flt. Lt. Albert L. Womersley and serial N7216 flown by Fg. Off. John R. Hollington. They brought back photographs taken from 18,000 ft but Hollington was engaged in an air battle with three Arado AR68 fighters, without casualties on either side. At this early stage in the war, the RAF was not equipped with specialized long-distance aircraft capable of photography at very high altitude. Eight days later, Bomber Command despatched eleven Hampdens to bomb two destroyers in Heligoland but five aircraft were shot down and all the bombs missed the targets.
Ref: AIR 28/828

This Dornier Do18D flying boat, radio code K6+DL works number 0801, of 3/Küstenfliegergruppe 406, landed heavily in the North Sea on 10 November 1939 after an air battle with two Hudsons of 220 Squadron from Thornaby, flown by Sgt. Kenneth F. Scotney and Flt. Lt. Harold W.A. Sheahen. It then turned over and sank. Sheahen's Hudson was hit in the engagement and he flew it back to Thornaby. The second pilot in Scotney's Hudson, Sgt. Alfred C. Culver, took over the controls and attacked a second Dornier flying boat in the same position. This flying boat disappeared into the clouds after being hit. Oberleutnant zur See Lütjens was killed in the downed Dornier, but the remaining crew members were picked up by Dutch vessels.
Ref: AIR 28/828

The mainstay of Coastal Command at the outbreak of the Second World War was the Avro Anson I, with which nine of its sixteen squadrons were equipped. Although the Anson was considered an advanced machine when first introduced in March 1936, it was already obsolescent by September 1939. The radius of action was only 330 miles, the armament consisted of only one machine-gun in a manually operated turret and another firing forward, and it could carry only 330 lb of bombs. Nevertheless, Ansons gave very good accounts of themselves until replaced by Lockheed Hudsons and Bristol Beauforts. They were highly reliable and continued in RAF service as trainers and communications aircraft until being retired in June 1968. This photograph is of the prototype, serial K4771.
Ref: AIR 2/1511

In early 1940, a watch was kept by Coastal Command aircraft for the German fleet auxiliary *Altmark*, which was known by British Intelligence to be heading for Germany with numerous British seamen as prisoners. This suspicious-looking vessel was spotted in the North Atlantic at 12.55 hours on 2 January 1940 by the crew of Anson I serial K8766 flown from St Eval on a convoy escort by Plt. Off. Thomas F. Kerr of 217 Squadron. However, it was soon discovered that she was the Dutch *Tarn* of 6,850 tons. The real *Altmark* was located in Norwegian waters on 16 February 1940 by two Hudsons of 220 Squadron based at Thornaby. The destroyer HMS *Cossack* was laid alongside her and a naval boarding party rescued all the seamen, after some resistance.
Ref: AIR 27/1346

The British merchant tanker *Caroni River* of 7,807 tons hit a mine outside Falmouth on 20 January 1940, having left the harbour for trials while in ballast. She sank, although all her crew were saved. The photograph was taken from an Anson I of 217 Squadron based at St Eval.
Ref: AIR 28/733

The British merchant vessel *Protesilaus* of 9,577 tons was damaged by a mine not far from Mumbles Head on 22 January 1940 while in ballast en route from Liverpool to Barry. She began to sink by the stern and was taken in tow by tugs, as photographed in the afternoon from an Anson I of 217 Squadron based at St Eval. She was beached in Swansea Bay where she was partially repaired before being taken on 20 July to Briton Ferry in West Glamorgan. She arrived at Greenock on 27 August. On 13 September, while under tow to Scapa Flow to act as a blockship, she sprang a leak not far from Skerryvore Lighthouse in the Hebrides and began to sink once more. She was finished off by gunfire.
Ref: AIR 28/733

This neutral Norwegian merchant vessel, *Faro* of 844 tons, was torpedoed on 27 January 1940 about 15 miles north-east of Copinsay Light in the Orkneys during extensive operations by U-boats in the North Sea. She had left Sarpsborg near Oslo, in ballast, and was bound for Methil in the Firth of Forth. Of her crew, seven were lost and eight saved. The stricken vessel drifted ashore at Taracliff Bay in the Orkneys and became a total loss. The photograph was taken from 300 ft at 13.14 hours on 28 January from Anson I serial N9673 of 269 Squadron, flown by Flt. Lt. Charles D.W. Price and based at Wick, during a hunt for the ship's lifeboat.
Ref: AIR 28/941

The British tanker *Greatfield* of 10,191 tons, laden with 13,000 tons of oil fuel and bound for Invergordon from Curaçao, was torpedoed by a U-boat south-west of Wick on 14 February 1940. This photograph was taken at midday from 500 ft by Hudson I serial N7272 of 224 Squadron from Leuchars, flown by Plt. Off. Hugh F. O'Neill. The crew of the Hudson collaborated with a British destroyer in the vicinity, but the tanker remained on fire and gradually drifted ashore near Dunbeath. Eleven of her forty-one crew were lost. She broke in two on 19 March and became a total loss.
Ref: AIR 28/470

This Anson I of 269 Squadron, serial N9673, came to grief when taking off down-wind at Wick on 21 March 1940. No one was badly injured but the aircraft was written off.
Ref: AIR 27/1568

During the evening of 8 April 1940, two Hurricane Is of 43 Squadron, based temporarily at Wick for defensive duties under the control of Coastal Command, were on patrol when they encountered two enemy aircraft about 30 miles east of Duncansby Head. Sgt. Herbert J.L. Hallowes fired all his ammunition into this Heinkel He111H-3, radio code 1H+DP works number 5614 of 6/Kampfgeschwader 26, which disappeared into low cloud below, obviously in difficulties. Hallowes prudently remained above cloud. About ten minutes after the engagement, the Heinkel circled the flarepath at Wick, with one engine out of action, and then crash-landed. The pilot, Leutnant K. Weigel, and the air observer, Oberfeldwebel B. Rehbein, were uninjured and taken prisoner. The Heinkel was riddled with bullets and the two gunners, Oberfeldwebel E. Rost and Oberfeldwebel K. Geerdts, were dead. The pilot said that he thought he was above a seaplane base when he circled the flarepath.
Ref: AIR 27/1568

From 9 April 1940, Coastal Command was actively engaged in reconnaissance of the German naval and airborne forces which were invading Norway. This photograph of Bergen was taken at 06.00 hours on 10 April from Hudson I serial N7324 of 233 Squadron from Leuchars, flown by Fg. Off. Henry E. Hopkins. He flew at 1,000 ft near the port and over the surrounding fjord. The crew reported thirty merchant vessels and twelve flying boats, as well as one enemy cruiser which opened up intense flak. Fire was also aimed at the Hudson from machine-gun posts on hills around Bergen, but it returned safely to Leuchars.
Ref: AIR 28/470

Another reconnaissance took place later in the morning of 10 April 1940 when Flt. Lt. Andrew H. McLaren flew Hudson I serial N7280 of 233 Squadron from Leuchars to Stavanger. Thirty-three medium and three large enemy aircraft were located on the airport, which was photographed from 11,000 ft.
Ref: AIR 28/470

McLaren then flew on to Haugesund, where ten merchant vessels were photographed from 1,000 ft and a Swedish merchant vessel was seen moving up the sound. The Hudson returned safely.
Ref: AIR 28/470

In the morning of 12 April 1940, Plt. Off. Laurence G. Nolan-Neylan flew Hudson I serial N7217 of 224 Squadron from Leuchars on a reconnaissance over the area of Hardangerfjord. In Bommelfjord the crew found two German merchant vessels and were fired upon. There were eleven merchant vessels in Lervis harbour and one in Aalfjord. Five more were located in Avaldsnes, which was photographed at 12.55 hours from 800 ft, as shown here.
Ref: AIR 28/470

Continuing the reconnaissance, Nolan-Neylan flew south to Kopervic, where thirteen merchant vessels were seen. This photograph of Haugesund was taken from 800 ft at 13.20 hours, but a round from a machine-gun pierced an engine cooler and Nolan-Neylan flew back to Leuchars on one engine.
Ref: AIR 28/470

In the morning of 13 April 1940, Flt. Lt. Harold W.A. Sheahen flew a Hudson of 220 Squadron on a reconnaissance of the Norwegian coast between Oberstad and Kristiansand. Photographs of Junkers Ju52 seaplanes on shallow water were taken at the seaplane base near Stavanger airport.
Ref: AIR 28/828

During the reconnaissance, Sheahen's Hudson was attacked at 10.16 hours by a Messerschmitt Bf110 when at 1,000 ft near Stavanger airport. The enemy aircraft made four attacks, damaging the rear turret of the Hudson on the second occasion. In the fourth attack the rear gunner, Plt. Off. William E. Nicholas, was put out of action by wounds in an arm and hand. However, dense smoke was seen to be coming from an engine of the Bf110, which then dived towards the sea in flames. The Hudson returned safely.
Ref: AIR 28/828

On 15 April 1940, Plt. Off. David Lingwood flew a Hudson I of 220 Squadron from Thornaby on a patrol off southern Norway. He was recalled after reaching Lillesand, where six merchant vessels were spotted and several photographs taken. After leaving this port, he was attacked twice by two Messerschmitt Bf110s but managed to escape in cloud. Then he came across two German destroyers and made several attacks but was foiled by low cloud and intense flak which damaged the Hudson. Nevertheless he brought the aircraft back to Thornaby with the photographs of Lillesand.
Ref: AIR 28/828

On 10 May 1940, a Hudson of 233 Squadron was flown by Sgt. William L. Ather from Leuchars to Boknafjord, south of Stavanger, where many merchant vessels were seen, including those in this photograph. Ather continued the reconnaissance as far as Stavanger, where the Hudson came under heavy flak. It was not hit, however, and returned safely.
Ref: AIR 28/470

On 11 and 12 May 1940, 'battle flights' of three Hudsons apiece were sent out from Leuchars and Thornaby to protect the crippled destroyer *Kelly* of 1,695 tons, commanded by Captain Lord Louis Mountbatten. Earlier, four German minelayers escorted by three destroyers and a flotilla of five motor-torpedo boats had been laying mines off the Great Fisher Bank in the North Sea, and the Royal Navy had despatched a cruiser and seven destroyers to intercept them. In very bad weather shortly before midnight on 9 May, *Kelly* had been hit by a torpedo fired by the MTB *S-31*, which then collided with her. The damaged destroyer had been taken in tow by the destroyer HMS *Bulldog*, but in the morning of 11 May the tow was taken over by the destroyer HMS *Fury*, as shown in this photograph taken by a Hudson of 233 Squadron from Leuchars. The Hudsons drove off an intruding Heinkel He111.
Ref: AIR 28/470

HMS *Kelly* under tow on 12 May, photographed by a Hudson of 220 Squadron from Thornaby while escorting her towards the Tyne.
Ref: AIR 28/828

The badly damaged HMS *Kelly* photographed after she berthed at Hebburn-on-Tyne in the early evening of 13 May 1940.
Ref: ADM 199/905

The German attack in the West, which began with the invasion of the neutral Low Countries on 10 May 1940, was followed by the capitulation of the Netherlands four days later. In the morning of 18 May, the Dutch merchant vessel *Confid*, of 249 tons, was photographed while entering the Humber Estuary by Hudson I serial N7343 of 206 Squadron from Bircham Newton in Norfolk, flown by Flt. Sgt. Geoffrey A. Turner. On the night of 18/19 May, Turner was killed in action during a raid on Hamburg.
Ref: AIR 28/75

This open boat, with about fifteen British soldiers on board, was sighted off Ostend at 05.26 hours on 25 May 1940 by an Anson of 500 Squadron based at Detling in Kent and flown by Sgt. Freestone. A British destroyer was located about ten minutes later and guided to the rescue.
Ref: AIR 28/75

On 29 May 1940, Sqn. Ldr. Terence H. Carr of 220 Squadron led a flight of Hudsons from Bircham Newton on a patrol off the Belgian and French coasts. The crews reported heavy bombing of Dunkirk, including attacks on a hospital ship, gas works and oil tanks.
Ref: AIR 28/75

On 31 May 1940, Plt. Off. Charles T. Dacombe flew a Hudson of 220 Squadron on a patrol off IJmuiden. The Dutch had sunk the old liner *Jan Pieterszoon Coen* of 11,140 tons as a blockship in the harbour entrance and submerged an old minesweeper behind her. The passenger ship *Van Rehsselaer* of 4,191 tons, which had been damaged by a mine, was grounded by the south pier, while the merchant vessel *Naaldwick* of 2,041 tons was sunk at the locks entrance.
Ref: AIR 28/75

Continuing his patrol down the Dutch coast, Dacombe passed this Junkers Ju52 stranded on a beach, probably part of the broad dunes off Wassenaar. On 10 May 1940, the Luftwaffe had landed over twenty-five of these transports carrying airborne soldiers on the beaches, since they were unable to land on airfields. Only five were able to take off again. Blenheims of Bomber Command attacked some of the remainder and German sources record that nine of them were destroyed.
Ref: AIR 28/75

In the early morning of 1 June 1940, Plt. Off. Goronwy Edwards of 233 Squadron flew Hudson I serial N7244 from Leuchars to Bergen on a meteorological reconnaissance. The aircrew reported about fifty merchant vessels moored around the quay, one of which fired at the Hudson without result. Edwards then dropped three 250 lb general-purpose bombs on two oil tanks but they overshot.
Ref: AIR 28/471

At the outbreak of the Second World War, only two Coastal Command squadrons were equipped with the Short Sunderland, which had first entered squadron service in June 1938 as a long-range flying boat employed on general reconnaissance and anti-submarine work. This prototype, serial K4774, was photographed during a test while loaded to its all-up weight of 56,000 lb. Heavily armed with four machine-guns in each of the nose and tail turrets and two more on the beams, it was named the 'Flying Porcupine' by the Germans. It gave excellent service throughout the war and beyond.
Ref: AIR 2/2928

On the morning of 3 June 1940, Sqn. Ldr. Douglas W. Lydall led three Hudson Is of 220 Squadron from Bircham Newton to reconnoitre Dunkirk, where fires were burning fiercely and the rearguard of the Army was still holding out. The evacuation ended during the following morning, by which time 335,490 men had been rescued by the Royal Navy and a flotilla of small ships manned by civilian volunteers. Ref: AIR 28/75

On 23 June 1940, Sunderland I serial P9600 of 10 (RAAF) Squadron from Mount Batten, with Flt. Lt. E.B. Courtney as captain and Fg. Off. H.G. Havyatt as first pilot, was escorting a convoy about 300 miles west of Ushant. In the afternoon, the crew spotted a lifeboat containing about twenty men from a torpedoed ship.
Ref: AIR 27/149

One of the ships in the convoy, the French merchant vessel *Cap Cantin* of 3,317 tons, was directed from its course to the position of the lifeboat. The Sunderland remained in the area until the men in the lifeboat had been taken off, in very rough seas. The Sunderland then continued to escort the convoy, eventually returning to Mount Batten after a flight of almost eleven hours.
Ref: AIR 27/149

The Norwegian merchant tanker *Eli Knudsen* of 9,026 tons was torpedoed by a U-boat about 150 miles west of Land's End on 23 June 1940, while carrying 9,000 tons of diesel and 3,000 tons of fuel oil from Aruba to Swansea. She sank after being taken in tow, but her crew of thirty-seven was saved. The photograph was taken from an Anson I of 217 Squadron, based at St Eval, while on convoy escort duties.
Ref: AIR 28/733

TAKE ARMS
JULY 1940 – JUNE 1941

After a few short weeks of German aggression, Coastal Command faced an enemy coastline which stretched from the North Cape of Norway to the Franco-Spanish border. This increase in the Command's responsibilities was colossal. Within this vast coastline lay superb ports and anchorages which could harbour enemy surface vessels as well as provide bases for U-boats hunting British convoys bringing vital supplies from around the world, particularly across the North Atlantic. For the next year, Britain with her Commonwealth and Empire fought the enemy alone.

Yet Coastal Command was unable to expand rapidly, mainly because Britain's limited resources were devoted to defence against an invasion which seemed imminent. The precursor to such an invasion was German air superiority and the only way to prevent this was to concentrate on expanding Fighter Command, with Bomber Command as a second priority in the attempts to reduce Germany's capacity to wage war. Nevertheless, some improvements in the strength of Coastal Command did take place, partly as a result of measures already in force before the collapse of the West. Hudsons steadily took the place of Ansons, although some of the latter still soldiered on in front-line squadrons. More Sunderlands arrived, replacing the older types of flying boats. The new Beaufort torpedo-bomber, which suffered technical faults when it entered service in late 1939, was reintroduced in the course of 1940. Blenheim IVs, which were being phased out of Bomber Command, were transferred to Coastal Command. Whitleys had also become obsolescent in Bomber Command and some were transferred, together with a few Wellingtons which were then fitted with the new Air to Surface-Vessel (ASV) radar. A single squadron was equipped with Beaufighter ICs in December 1940; this type of aircraft would play a major part in the Command's successes in the future. Some Swordfish squadrons of the Fleet Air Arm were placed under the control of the Command, becoming land-based. Photo-reconnaissance Spitfires and Hudsons were allocated to the Command. By the end of 1940, the strength of Coastal Command had increased to 554 aircraft, although this rate of expansion was well below that of the other Commands.

The tasks faced by the squadrons appeared insuperable. Sinkings of merchant vessels by U-boats reached appalling levels, threatening the very existence of Britain. The U-boat commanders described this period as 'The Happy Time'. They were able to operate in a stretch in the middle of the North Atlantic which was beyond the range of RAF aircraft, even though British forces had landed in Iceland in May 1940 and secured the country as an air base. Winston Churchill later confessed that these U-boat successes were the only matter which caused him to wonder if Britain could prevail in the war.

The surface warships of the Kriegsmarine were also powerful, with great battleships and cruisers, supported by destroyers, torpedo boats, minesweepers and smaller craft. Germany had commandeered a huge merchant fleet from the conquered countries. Added to its own fleet, this plied along the coasts of Europe, heavily protected by armed trawlers and other escort vessels. One of the main purposes was to bring high-grade iron ore from Sweden via Narvik and Rotterdam, from where it was transported by barge to the Ruhr, the centre of Germany's war industry.

These were the enemies which Coastal Command faced in the year following the fall of France. Yet even in these 'dark days', there were glimmers of hope. The battleship *Gneisenau* was torpedoed and badly damaged in Brest harbour by a single Beaufort on 6 April 1941. A similar fate befell the battle cruiser *Lützow* on 13 June 1941 off south-west Norway. However, direct air attacks against enemy convoys proved very costly for Coastal Command, and the operations were interspersed with minelaying near the entrance of enemy ports. Magnetic mines were dropped from low level and lay on the sea bottom, where they could be activated by the steel hulls of vessels passing above. Minelaying produced significant results for far smaller losses in terms of aircrews and aircraft. In addition, the light bombers of the Command made frequent night attacks against enemy ports.

Meanwhile, British science and ingenuity were coming to the aid of the hard-pressed crews. Airborne depth charges were produced, although Coastal Command accounted for only a single U-boat during this year. The ASV radar sets were still rudimentary, but more advanced equipment was in production. The Government Code and Cypher School at Bletchley Park was beginning to decrypt the wireless traffic of the Kriegsmarine in home waters. The Coastal Command Development Unit, set up in November 1940, was carrying out trials with new equipment and devising new tactics for both anti-submarine and anti-shipping operations. On the global front, Germany attacked Russia on 22 June 1941, and the war entered a new phase.

Overleaf: Bristol Blenheim IVs were introduced into Coastal Command in January 1940, superseding the short-nose Blenheim Is. They were employed on shipping protection work around the coasts but some were fitted with four-gun packs beneath the fuselage, in addition to the single machine-gun in the wing and the two in the turret, and called Blenheim IVFs. They were classed as 'long-range fighters' and continued in this role until replaced by Bristol Beaufighters armed with cannons. This photograph shows a Blenheim IV, serial N6212, which was one of the first to be built.
Ref: SUPP 9/1

A gun pack beneath the fuselage of a Blenheim IVF was modified by Coastal Command in January 1941 to take two Hispano 20-mm cannons. However, the normal armament in the pack was four .303-in Browning machine-guns.
Ref: AIR 15/560

An Anson I of 217 Squadron serial K8782, flown by Plt. Off. Frank A. Tams from St Eval, came across this sinking tanker at mid-morning on 7 July 1940, while on convoy escort duties about 200 miles west of the Scilly Islands. The vessel was on fire and the crew took to the lifeboats. The aircraft flew at 1,000 ft, in good weather over a calm sea. It was thought at the time that the vessel was French, but Lloyds' records indicate that she was the Dutch tanker *Lucretia* of 2,584 tons, torpedoed by a U-boat in this position while carrying a cargo of gas oil from Aruba to Avonmouth. Two of her crew were killed but thirty were saved.
Ref: AIR 28/733

Daylight reconnaissance could be extremely hazardous in the Bristol Blenheim IVs of 53 Squadron, which were outclassed by enemy fighters. At 11.30 hours on 18 July 1940 this photograph of Boulogne harbour, one of the invasion ports, was taken from 3,000 ft by a Blenheim flown from Detling in Kent by Plt. Off. Harold M. Newton. The aircraft was pursued by a Messerschmitt Bf109 when three-quarters of the way back over the English Channel. The gunner in the Blenheim opened fire on the enemy from 500 yd, while Newton took evasive action and managed to return safely.
Ref: CN 5/13

In the afternoon of 22 July 1940, Plt. Off. David B. Starky flew a Hudson of 53 Squadron from Detling in Kent to photograph the docks at Dunkirk from 3,000 ft. He continued to Gravelines and returned from a successful photo-reconnaissance. Starky did not return from another sortie three days later, when he and his crew lost their lives.
Ref: CN 5/13

During the afternoon of 19 August 1940, two German aircraft flew over the RAF's flying boat base at Pembroke Dock and dropped bombs on Llanheath oil tanks nearby. Eight of the fifteen tanks, each containing 12,000 tons of fuel, were set ablaze. The fire was brought under control during the following night. This photograph was taken on 19 August from an Anson of 217 Squadron, probably on detachment at Carew Cheriton in Pembrokeshire.
Ref: AIR 28/733

At 13.50 hours on 21 August 1940, two Junkers Ju88s dropped sticks of bombs from low level on St Eval airfield. These destroyed No. 4 hangar, damaged No. 3 hangar, and hit 217 Squadron's car park between the hangars and destroyed a Standard 8. No casualties were recorded. Three Blenheim IV fighters of 236 Squadron had just taken off on escort duties and attacked one of the enemy aircraft, chasing it down to Land's End where it escaped in cloud. Three more took off a few minutes later and fired at the other enemy aircraft, without visible effect, but it escaped into cloud over Padstow. The airmen in this photograph, taken outside No. 4 hangar on the same day of the raid, seem interested but unperturbed.
Ref: AIR 28/733

This burning merchant vessel was photographed at dusk on 3 September 1940 about 20 miles east of Aberdeen when four Hudsons of 224 Squadron flew on a patrol from Leuchars. She was the British merchant vessel *St Glen* of 4,647 tons, which had been attacked by a German aircraft while en route to Hull from Rosario and Buenos Aires laden with 4,900 tons of wheat, 1,339 tons of canned beef, 984 tons of salted hides and 221 tons of general cargo. Three of her crew of forty-three were lost, and she sank three days later. Ref: AIR 28/471

The British merchant vessel *Harpenden* of 4,678 tons was hit in the stern by a torpedo from a U-boat on 11 September 1940, while sailing without cargo in convoy from Hull to St Lawrence. One crew member was lost. Sunderland I serial P9603 of 10 (RAAF) Squadron, on detachment at Oban in Argyllshire and captained by Flt. Lt. J.A. Cohen, arrived over her at 08.57 hours, about 350 miles out in the North Atlantic. The Sunderland was ordered to remain on station to the limit of its endurance and was not waterborne at base until 18.40 hours, 13 hours 35 minutes after take-off. Meanwhile, *Harpenden* was taken in tow. She arrived in the Clyde eventually and was beached, before being taken to Greenock for repair. Ref: AIR 27/149

The Blackburn Botha must rank as one of the least successful aircraft produced for the RAF during the Second World War. It was designed as a reconnaissance aircraft and torpedo-bomber with a crew of four, intended to replace Ansons in some Coastal Command squadrons. It first entered service with 608 Squadron at Thornaby during June 1940 but proved both underpowered and unresponsive at the controls.

The first operational flight was made on 10 August and the last on 6 November 1940. No other squadron was equipped with Bothas and all aircraft were transferred to training duties, a few continuing in service until September 1944. This photograph of the first prototype, serial L6104, was taken on 22 May 1939.
Ref: AIR 2/5151

On 5 October 1940, the Dutch merchant vessel *Ottoland* of 2,202 tons was en route from Buctouche in New Brunswick to Immingham in Lincolnshire when she struck a mine about four miles off Hartlepool. She was carrying pit props in her hold and a deck cargo of timber. Plt. Off. Richard W. Pye of 608 Squadron took off from Thornaby at 09.55 hours in Anson I serial N5197, to render assistance. The vessel was found in a sinking condition but minesweepers were directed to her position and all crew members were saved. This photograph was taken after the rescue, when the ship was going down and her cargo was floating away.
Ref: AIR 28/828

The Bristol Beaufort entered service with Coastal Command in November 1939, superseding obsolescent Vickers Vildebeest biplanes as 'the world's fastest torpedo bomber'. The machines suffered at first from mechanical problems and, with a crew of four, were somewhat underpowered and inadequately armed. From April 1940, they were engaged mainly on minelaying and as light bombers. When sorties with torpedoes began in September 1940, the Beaufort squadrons suffered the heaviest casualties of all RAF squadrons in the Second World War. Nevertheless they gave excellent service with Coastal Command until they began to be withdrawn in June 1942 and flown to the Mediterranean theatre. This photograph was taken in November 1942 at Sidney in Vancouver Island, where 32 Operational Training Unit was based. The aircraft was probably Beaufort I serial N1005, which was handed over in that month to the newly formed 149 Squadron of the RCAF for operations in the Pacific theatre.
Ref: AIR 29/676

Torpedo attacks by Beauforts of 22 Squadron, based at North Coates in Lincolnshire, began in September 1940. They usually took the form of daylight 'Rover' patrols off the Dutch coast and the Frisian Islands, and several enemy ships were sunk or damaged. This photograph of the German merchant vessel *Moltkefels* of 7,860 tons was taken on 29 November 1940, when a Beaufort came across an enemy convoy off Terschelling at 15.00 hours. The pilot attacked but his torpedo missed and he went back to rearm. Meanwhile, two other Beauforts took off and it was believed that one of their torpedoes hit this vessel. All aircraft returned, in spite of intense flak. There are no German records of ships sunk or damaged on this occasion. It is possible that the water was too shallow and the torpedoes were exploding on underwater sandbanks.

Ref: AIR 28/595

A Beaufort of 22 Squadron, flown from North Coates by Flt. Lt. A.H. Richard Beauman, came across this enemy merchant vessel in the early afternoon of 1 December 1940, while on a Rover Patrol off the German Frisian Islands. It was the Finnish *Rigel* of 3,773 tons, under German control. He dropped his torpedo but it dived into the water when the drum control gear, designed to ensure that it entered the water at the correct angle, caught in the gunner's harness. Beauman returned safely on this occasion but was shot down four days later. He and his crew lost their lives.

Ref: AIR 28/595

On 27 December 1940, three Beauforts of 22 Squadron which took off at 10.30 hours on a Rover patrol from North Coates came across two enemy merchant vessels off the Dutch island of Terschelling. All three dropped torpedoes but they missed. Three more Beauforts took off at 15.30 hours to attack the same target, arriving at dusk. Two did not attack owing to poor visibility. The other, flown by Sqn. Ldr. Dennis V.W. Francis, did not return and he and his crew lost their lives. German records show that *Sperrbrecher 17*, the merchant vessel *Templar* of 6,728 tons converted into a minesweeper and heavily-armed escort, was badly damaged at this time. Thus it appears that Francis torpedoed this ship before being shot down. This photograph was taken during the earlier attack.
Ref: AIR 28/595

The photograph is unusual since it shows an Italian submarine in the North Atlantic. The *Bagnolini* of 1,166 tons was one of six Italian submarines sent to Bordeaux in late 1940 and assigned to an area west of Ireland, to help the Germans in their U-boat war against Britain. After being damaged by depth charges during an attack on a convoy, she was returning on the surface to Bordeaux when, at 17.30 hours on 3 January 1941, the crew of a Beaufort I of 217 Squadron based at St Eval spotted her about 350 miles west of La Rochelle. The aircraft was flown by a New Zealander serving in the RAF, Flt. Lt. A. Victor Hunter, who was looking for a German tanker. He straddled the submarine with four 250 lb semi-armour piercing bombs, which missed narrowly. The Beaufort crew then fired all their ammunition at the submarine, but the bullets made no impression on the hull, while the submarine returned fire. Hunter returned to St Eval and the *Bagnolini* put into St Jean de Luz two days later.
Ref: AIR 28/733

At 13.25 hours on 17 January 1941, four Beauforts of 22 Squadron from North Coates, escorted by three Blenheim IVFs of 235 Squadron from Bircham Newton, attacked an enemy convoy off IJmuiden. Each Beaufort dropped six 250 lb general-purpose bombs while the Blenheims machine-gunned the decks of the vessels. There was no serious damage to the ships but two Beauforts were hit by accurate light flak. All aircraft returned safely, although the Beaufort crews thought that one Blenheim had been shot down. This photograph of an enemy merchant vessel was taken from one of the Beauforts.
Ref: AIR 28/595

On 25 January 1941, three Beauforts of 22 Squadron from North Coates encountered a German convoy off Scheveningen. One Beaufort was carrying a torpedo while the others carried two 500 lb and two 250 lb general-purpose bombs. The torpedo was aimed at the largest vessel but missed. Another Beaufort, flown by Fg. Off. Donald C. Sharman, was hit by flak and crash-landed near Bircham Newton. Ref: AIR 28/595

The British merchant tanker *W.B. Walker* of 10,468 tons was torpedoed by a U-boat on 29 January 1941, while sailing from Halifax to Avonmouth. She had been loaded with 13,338 tons of aviation and pool spirit at Aruba. Sunderland I serial T9047 of 10 (RAAF) Squadron, flown from Oban in Argyllshire by Flt. Lt. J.P. Costello, arrived over her at 15.50 hours, about 350 miles out in the North Atlantic. The tanker broke in two but the parts continued to float for a while. Four crew members were killed. Costello remained over the scene as long as possible, but was forced by bad weather on his return to put down at Inverness at 23.35 hours, out of fuel. Ref: AIR 27/150

On 5 March 1941, two Beauforts of 22 Squadron from North Coates attacked the Danish merchant vessel *Uffe* of 1,889 tons, which was under German control, south of Heligoland. Fg. Off. James R. Hyde dropped a torpedo, but it ran short and sank. Plt. Off. Kenneth Campbell bombed the ship but missed. Hyde's crew machine-gunned the decks and the ship's crew began to abandon the vessel, as can be seen in this photograph, although no serious damage was caused. A month later, in the early morning of 6 April 1941, Campbell flew Beaufort I serial N1016 of 22 Squadron from St Eval over the outer harbour of Brest, where the German battleship *Gneisenau* of 31,850 tons was at anchor. His torpedo blew a 40-ft hole in the side of the battleship, which almost sank and was out of commission for five months. The Beaufort was shot down by fire from the mole and all crew members lost their lives. Campbell was awarded a posthumous Victoria Cross.
Ref: AIR 28/595

On 23 May 1941, a daylight raid by Beauforts on Lanveoc airfield, near Brest, was contemplated by 217 Squadron at St Eval, but No. 19 Group decided to allow only one aircraft to go. Plt. Off. Edward A. Rance and his crew volunteered but found there was no cloud cover when they neared the target. Rance decided to continue down the coast and bombed an 'Altmark' tanker in the roads of La Pallice. The crew believed that a direct hit was scored but there are no German records of any damage.
Ref: AIR 28/733

A Beaufort of 217 Squadron from St Eval, flown by Fg. Off. Thomas S. Kitching, made an attack on La Pallice in the morning of 9 June 1941. Circling down from 2,000 ft, a stick of 250 lb general-purpose bombs was released at 100 ft over a merchant vessel estimated as 450 ft in length. The gunner then fired 80 rounds into buildings on the wharf. However, there are no German records of any damage to a merchant vessel at this time.
Ref: AIR 28/733

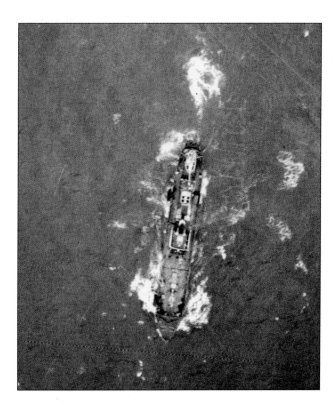

On 9 June 1941, Plt. Off. A.N. Jacob flew a Blenheim IV of 53 Squadron from St Eval to the Bay of Biscay, where he attacked a merchant vessel of about 2,000 tons. Two 250 lb general-purpose bombs were dropped from 200 ft and two more from 600 ft, but each salvo missed by about 40 ft.
Ref: AIR 28/733

The only RAF unit to be equipped with Northrop N3P-B floatplanes was 330 (Norwegian) Squadron, which received eighteen of these machines from June 1941 when based at Reykjavik in Iceland. They were employed on convoy escort duties until replaced by Catalina flying boats from June 1942. A few continued in service until January 1943. This photograph was taken on 24 November 1941 from a Hudson of 269 Squadron based at Kaldadarnes in Iceland.
Ref: AIR 27/1568

In the late afternoon of 10 June 1941 a fire broke out in Sunderland I serial N9047 of 204 Squadron at Skerjafordur, near Reykjavik in Iceland. The squadron had moved to this base on 5 April 1941, from Sullom Voe in the Shetlands. The Sunderland had alighted an hour before and was being refuelled at her moorings. Some of her crew had already gone ashore and the remainder were taken off unharmed by motor launch. Within seven minutes, the flying boat had burnt out and was two-thirds under water. Oil was still burning on the water when this photograph was taken from the salvage vessel *Manela*.
Ref: CN 5/14

Overnight salvage work was begun and by the following morning the four engines had been recovered. The fire had not reached these. By 14 June the mooring had been cleared of the remaining wreckage. Ref: CN 5/14

A Sea of Troubles
July 1941 – June 1942

By the middle of 1941, Coastal Command was still unable to carry out successfully all the tasks it faced. Its establishment of Sunderlands, Whitleys, Hudsons, Beauforts, Beaufighters and PR aircraft was increasing steadily, while Blenheims and Ansons were being phased out. Meteorological squadrons were being formed, making an unspectacular but invaluable contribution to the conduct of the air war in general. One encouraging development was the equipment of a single squadron with B-24 Liberators at this time, which began to close the 'Atlantic Gap' by operating from Northern Ireland. Another entrant was the Catalina, which became more numerous after entering RAF service three months earlier. Although slow, this flying boat was well armed and reliable, with a very long endurance which enabled it to carry out excellent service for the remainder of the war.

However, the squadrons were still hard-pressed and short of the equipment which would ultimately bring victory. There were a few successes against U-boats and attacks against enemy coastal convoys resulted in some sinkings. Of course, the progress of the war was transformed when Germany unwisely declared war on the USA after the Japanese attacked Pearl Harbor on 6 December 1941. This did not bring the immediate participation of the USAAF or the USNAF into the European theatre, but it ensured that the vast potential of American aircraft production would be ranged against the enemy. Moreover, there could no longer be any doubts about the successful outcome of the war.

By the end of 1941, the strength of Coastal Command stood at 633 aircraft and it was becoming a more formidable force. However, in February 1942 the Command shared in the general humiliation of the country when German battleships together with a cruiser, destroyers and torpedo boats made the 'Channel Dash' from Brest to German home waters, damaged only by mines laid by the RAF. This was in spite of an immense effort by both Bomber and Coastal Commands in very adverse weather, during which many lives were lost.

In the spring of 1942, events in the Mediterranean and the rapid advance of the Japanese in the Far East to positions where their naval units could threaten India and Ceylon necessitated the gradual withdrawal of all the Beaufort squadrons from Britain to these theatres of war. By May, Coastal Command was almost bereft of torpedo-bombers. Hampdens, no longer required by Bomber Command, were converted to take their place. These aircraft carried out some excellent work but they constituted only a stop-gap, for the formidable Beaufighter was also being adapted to perform this role. Meanwhile, the task of minelaying had been largely taken over by Bomber Command and there were numerous sinkings of enemy vessels from its operations, particularly in the Baltic Sea which could be reached by heavy bombers.

In the course of the twelve months ending June 1942, Coastal Command sank eight U-boats or Italian submarines, of which two were shared with HM ships. Several more were damaged. This was not a remarkable success, but certain developments were bringing about a major transformation in the effectiveness of the Command's anti-submarine operations. The ASV radar was undergoing considerable improvements in its range and clarity. Depth charges were becoming more deadly, with pistols designed to explode near the surface when dropped over diving U-boats. Increasing numbers of long-range aircraft were closing the 'Atlantic Gap' and hindering the enemy's immunity from land-based air attack in this vital area. The Government Code and Cypher School was decrypting enemy signals to the point where the British were becoming aware of the approximate positions of all U-boats at sea as well as the movement of enemy coastal convoys.

In June 1942, a new device was employed operationally for the first time when an Italian U-boat was detected by ASV at night off the northern coast of Spain by a Wellington equipped with the new Leigh Light, which homed on to the target. The puzzled submariners were almost blinded by a sudden and dazzling light. Next, there followed unexpected and severe damage to their craft when depth charges were dropped and machine-guns opened up on them. The submarine managed to edge to safety in Spain, but this action heralded a new era in the anti-submarine war. Although the enemy did not yet fully realize what was in store, from this time on his submarines would be unable to travel on the surface at night with near-immunity. The night was the time when submarines relied on surfacing, taking in fresh air, recharging batteries and moving rapidly to or from their targets. All that was about to change. Moreover, the German coastal convoys were to experience some very unpleasant surprises within the next year.

The Consolidated Catalina flying boat, with a crew of up to nine and a range of about 4,000 miles, first entered service with Coastal Command in March 1941. In October of that year, torpedo trials were made with this Catalina II serial AM266 by the Torpedo Development Unit at Gosport. It was found that British 18-in torpedoes were suitable if they were fitted with controlled air rudders and anti-roll

gear. However, the Catalina was not used in this role but continued as a reconnaissance and anti-submarine aircraft until the end of the war.

Ref: AVIA 16/59

In the early morning of 27 July 1941, a Beaufort of 217 Squadron, flown by Plt. Off. Peter F.R. Graham, went out on a shipping strike in the Bay of Biscay. It came across a Heinkel He115 floatplane at 600 ft and an air combat ensued. Graham opened fire with his front gun from 150 yd, closing to 20 yd. His gunner, Sgt. Ralph Marshall, was also able to bring his turret to bear. The German rear gunner did not reply, indicating that he had been hit. The enemy aircraft dived to port and then gained cloud cover, breaking off the engagement. On 21 August 1941, Graham and his crew failed to return from another sortie and all four men lost their lives.
Ref: AIR 28/733

A remarkable success was scored by two Hudsons of 269 Squadron on 27 August 1941 while operating from Kaldadarnes in Iceland, having arrived at this base the previous April. One of the Hudsons, flown by Sqn. Ldr. J.H. Thompson, dropped depth charges at 10.50 hours on a U-boat surfaced about 150 miles south of Iceland and then machine-gunned the decks. The Hudson crew was surprised to see a white flag being waved from the conning tower and then more sailors holding up a large white board. Unknown to them, chlorine gas had escaped within the U-boat. The Hudson signalled for help and remained on station until Catalina serial AH553 of 209 Squadron, flown by Fg. Off. E.A. Jewiss, arrived at 13.45 hours from Reykjavik.
Ref: AIR 27/1568

At 17.45 hours, Catalina serial AH565 of 209 Squadron arrived from Reykjavik, flown by Flt. Lt. B. Lewin. British warships then appeared on the scene and Lt. H.B. Campbell of the trawler HMS *Kingston Agate* crossed in a life raft to accept surrender of the U-boat. This was *U-570*, a Type VIIC commanded by Kapitänleutnant Hans Joachim Rahmlow. It was towed to Iceland and yielded important intelligence information, later being recommissioned as HMS *Graph*. One of the German officers tried to escape from prisoner-of-war camp in Cumbria in an attempt to scuttle the submarine in Barrow-in-Furness, but was shot and killed by a guard.
Ref: AIR 27/1568

On 2 September 1941, three Beauforts of 22 Squadron, detached from Thorney Island in Sussex to Leuchars, were led by Wg. Cdr. John C. Mayhew to the coast of south-west Norway. They found two merchant vessels off Stavanger and in the face of very intense flak dropped torpedoes, all three of which were seen to hit and explode. The German *Oslebhausen* of 4,989 tons was set on fire and sank. The Beauforts were then attacked by five Messerschmitt Bf109s. Two returned safely to Leuchars after reaching cloud cover but the third, flown by Flt. Sgt. Duncan McTavish, failed to return. All four crew members lost their lives.
Ref: AIR 15/263

At 10.55 hours on 2 October 1941, Plt. Off. Geoffrey S. Turner took off from Leuchars in Beaufort serial L9874 of 42 Squadron on a patrol along the Norwegian coast. Two merchant vessels of about 2,000 tons and 1,000 tons were spotted off Bergen at 13.46 hours and a 500 lb general-purpose bomb with delay action was dropped on each from about 30 ft. The crew thought that the smaller was hit while the larger was possibly hit, but there are no German records of any serious damage to vessels in the area on this day. The photograph is of the larger vessel, showing a miss astern. It was taken with an F24 camera mounted vertically, photographing through a mirror. Turner continued his patrol and dropped two 250 lb bombs on a factory and then machine-gunned a ship nearby. Although he returned safely from this sortie, he failed to return from another a fortnight later, when he and his crew lost their lives.
Ref: AIR 15/263

At 10.12 hours on 14 October 1941, Fg. Off. D.W. Passmore of 42 Squadron took off from Leuchars in Beaufort I serial L9874 for an anti-shipping patrol along the Norwegian coast. Two hours later, the crew spotted a merchant vessel west of Lister and attacked from 75 ft, dropping two 500 lb and two 250 lb bombs with eleven seconds delay. Hits were not observed but the ship's stern rose and then settled, leaving a large, oily patch astern while the crew took to white lifeboats. The Norwegian *Eros* of 974 tons sank.
Ref: AIR 15/263

At 10.55 hours on 22 October 1941, Whitley V serial T4329 of 612 Squadron, flown by Plt. Off. D.H. Limbrey, ditched with engine trouble about 40 miles off Land's End when returning to St Eval from a patrol over the Bay of Biscay. However, an SOS had been sent and Sunderland serial P9604 of 10 (RAAF) Squadron, captained by Flt. Lt. R.B. Burrage with Warr. Off. T.A. Egerton as 1st pilot, was diverted after having taken off from Pembroke Dock. During its hunt, the Sunderland received reports of a dinghy with five men aboard. It homed to the position by radar and jettisoned all bombs and depth charges before landing and taxiing towards it.
Ref: AIR 27/150

The five crew members of the Whitley were taken aboard the Sunderland, which then returned to Pembroke Dock, where it was waterborne at 20.00 hours. Both crews were then brought ashore by launch and photographed upon landing, in a relieved and happy mood.
Ref: AIR 27/150

Two Hudsons of 233 Squadron intercepted a Heinkel He111 about 425 miles west of Brest when on an anti-shipping patrol from St Eval on 3 November 1941. The first Hudson, serial AM575, flown by Fg. Off. Richard G. Winnicott, attacked from below 6,000 ft, opening fire with front guns at 800 yd and closing to 100 ft, when additional fire was opened from the turret. Tracer entered the whole length of the Heinkel, and its starboard engine caught fire while it dived to about 3,000 ft. The Hudson was hit in the wings, turret and rear fuselage by return fire. Winnicott broke off when his guns jammed. The attack was taken up by Hudson serial AM582 flown by Plt. Off. Wilson, who also riddled the Heinkel's fuselage with his front guns as it continued to dive. The tail of the Heinkel hit the sea but it recovered and turned for France at a slow speed. Wilson's Hudson was hit by incendiary bullets and both aircraft returned to Cornwall, where Wilson had to foreland at Portreath owing to petrol shortage.
Ref: AIR 28/733

On 27 November 1941, three Beauforts of 217 Squadron flew from Thorney Island to Coltishall in Norfolk for a daylight attack against enemy shipping off the Dutch coast. The pilot of the leading aircraft, Beaufort II serial AW248, was a Canadian in the RAF, Flt. Lt. John Percival, with the author as navigator. Escorted by six Spitfire IIAs of 152 Squadron, the formation took off at 09.30 hours and came across what appeared to be two merchant vessels and six armed trawlers off the Hook of Holland. The three Beauforts made diving attacks in turn on the leading vessel, each dropping two 500 lb and four 250 lb general-purpose bombs with eleven seconds delay. The vessel blew up and sank. German records show that she was the auxiliary defence vessel *HS.859*, formerly the Dutch *Delft* of 431 tons. Percival's aircraft was hit in the fuselage and starboard engine by a stream of bullets, one of which nicked his ankle, but a successful landing was made back at Coltishall.
Ref: AIR 15/263

In the afternoon of 23 November 1941, a German convoy was attacked south of Lister by Hudson T9396 of 320 (Dutch) Squadron, flown from Leuchars by Sgt.-Plt. C.A.E. van Otterloo. The target consisted of the Norwegian merchant ships *Ingerseks* of 4,969 tons and *Kong Ring* of 1,994 tons, escorted by the anti-submarine vessels *UJ.1405* and *UJ.1705*. Otterloo dived from cloud cover, firing from his front guns and dropping three 250 lb semi-armour piercing bombs with eleven seconds delay over *Ingerseks*. He then turned and fired at an escort vessel but 20-mm cannon shells riddled his cockpit and killed him. The captain/navigator, Off.-Plt. W.M.A. van Rossum, took over the controls and with the help of Off.-Navigator van der Meer, managed to right the Hudson and fly it back to Scotland. He landed at Wick, although he had never seen this airfield before and had no experience of flying a Hudson. All crew members were awarded the Vliegerkruis (the Dutch equivalent of the DFC or DFM). Although they thought they had scored a direct hit, the German records show that all three bombs missed narrowly. This photograph shows *Kong Ring*.
Ref: AIR 15/263

Three Beauforts of 217 Squadron from Manston in Kent took off in the afternoon of 9 December 1941 for an anti-shipping attack off the Dutch coast. Each aircraft was carrying four 500 lb general-purpose bombs with short delay fuses. They found a convoy of eight merchant vessels off IJmuiden and attacked the largest, the German *Madrid* of 8,777 tons, at low level. The first Beaufort, flown by Flt. Lt. Arthur J.H. Finch, hit the target amidships. The second, flown by Plt. Off. Mark Lee, was shot down and all crew members were killed. The third, flown by Plt. Off. Arthur H. Aldridge, hit the ship nearer the bows, although his port wingtip was sheared off by a bracing wire. The ship sank in shallow water, where it was photographed in February 1942.
Ref: AIR 15/263

No. 217 Squadron made its first torpedo attack in the afternoon of 16 December 1941 when three Beauforts flew from Thorney Island to Coltishall, where they were joined by three Beaufighters of 248 Squadron from Bircham Newton. Escorted by twelve Spitfire IIs of 152 Squadron and six Spitfire VBs of 19 Squadron, they headed for the Dutch coast and found a convoy of eight vessels and another of nine vessels off the Hook of Holland. They dropped their torpedoes against the one in this photograph but all missed, although one was thought to hit a flak ship. Explosions in the sea can also be seen in the

photograph. The Beaufighters raked the decks of several vessels with 20-mm cannon fire, causing much confusion. All aircraft returned, although one Beaufort was damaged by flak. Photo-interpreters thought that the vessel was the *Anna Maersk* of 5,300 tons but in fact she was the Norwegian *Knute Neilson* of 5,749 tons.

Ref: AIR 15/263

At 09.13 hours on 22 December 1941, Flt. Sgt. N. Carpenter took off from Wick in a Hudson of 220 Squadron for the Norwegian coast. The crew came across a tanker of about 5,000 tons and a merchant vessel of about 2,000 tons off Kristiansand, and attacked the tanker with four 250 lb general-purpose bombs at 11.53 hours. The attack was made from only 20 ft and the aircraft was slightly damaged from fouling a mast. Although the crew saw an explosion between the funnel and the bridge of the tanker, with wreckage thrown in the air, there are no German records of any serious damage to a vessel at this time and place.
Ref: AIR 15/263

On 23 December 1941, Sunderland I serial P9605 of 10 (RAAF) Squadron from Pembroke Dock, flown by Flt. Lt. V.A. Hodgkinson, found this tanker about 400 miles out in the North Atlantic. She gave a false name when challenged and Pembroke Dock ordered the Sunderland to attack. Hodgkinson dropped a stick of six depth charges and two anti-submarine bombs across her. Gunfire was exchanged and the Sunderland was holed below the waterline so that it had to be beached on return. The tanker was the German *Benno* of 8,306 tons, originally the Norwegian *Ole Jacob* which had left St Nazaire on 20 December 1941. Armed with one 105-mm gun and 20-mm flak guns, she was carrying a cargo of fuel oil and other provisions, with orders to refuel German surface raiders if required. Damaged by Hodgkinson's attack, she made for sanctuary in Spain.
Ref: AIR 15/263

Coastal Command began to receive Armstrong Whitley Vs in October 1940, when they had become obsolescent in Bomber Command squadrons. They were employed primarily on long-range reconnaissance against the increasing menace of U-boats, and performed a useful role although plagued with serviceability problems. This Whitley V serial Z9365 was fitted with long-range Air to Surface-Vessel radar (ASV) at the Royal Aircraft Establishment at Farnborough in July 1942. Such modified versions, which were also fitted with extra tankage, were known as Whitley GR VIIs.
Ref: AVIA 7/1493

The damaged tanker *Benno* was located at 10.28 hours on 24 December 1941 by a Whitley V of 502 Squadron on detachment at St Eval from Limavady in Northern Ireland. She was at anchor in an estuary at Puerto Cariño, near Cape Ortego in north-west Spain, as shown in this photograph. The Whitley did not attack but reported the discovery. At about 11.30 hours on the same day, three Beauforts of 22 Squadron were sent out from St Eval. One of these, flown by Plt. Off. James C. White, found the tanker and dropped a torpedo at 14.43 hours. This struck the vessel in the engine room abaft of amidships, killing one stoker. She began to sink by the stern, emitting a cloud of black smoke, while the Beaufort gunner raked the decks with machine-gun fire.
Ref: AIR 28/733

Shortly after the Beaufort left, Whitley VII serial Z9124 of 502 Squadron arrived from St Eval, flown by Plt. Off. Christopher Carmichael. The tanker had moved closer to the coast and settled in shallow water. Carmichael made two bombing runs, each with three 250 lb general-purpose bombs, while the crews exchanged gunfire. The tanker was destroyed. Soon afterwards, the Germans made indignant protests, accusing the British of violating international law, and the British responded by asserting that the vessel was outside the 3-mile limit (which was not correct). The incident soon blew over but the Germans lost an important supply vessel.
Ref: AIR 15/263

The Consolidated B-24C Liberator first entered service with Coastal Command in June 1941 as a 'Very Long Range' reconnaissance aircraft, intended to help close the gap in the middle of the North Atlantic which hitherto had not been covered by shore-based aircraft. The example in this photograph, a B-24D known in the RAF as a Liberator II, was fitted with power-operated turrets and employed in the bomber role. It was tested in April 1942 by the Air Fighting Development Unit at Duxford in Cambridgeshire. Liberator IIs were followed by other variants in Coastal Command. All were fitted with Air to Surface-Vessel radar and employed very effectively, primarily against U-boats.
Ref: AIR 16/933

There was an eventful day for the crew of Liberator I serial AM924 of 120 Squadron on 11 January 1942, when on detachment at St Eval from Nutts Corner in County Antrim. Flown by Fg. Off. Peter J. Cundy, the Liberator took off at 04.10 hours for a lengthy patrol over the Bay of Biscay. At 15.20 hours, when about 100 miles off the north-west tip of Spain, the crew saw a Heinkel He115 floatplane below and beneath them. Cundy banked to allow his rear and side gunners to open fire, at a distance of 200–600 yd. They scored numerous hits but the enemy aircraft disappeared in a rain squall. A U-boat and a merchant vessel were spotted about twenty minutes later, about 5 miles off the starboard beam. Cundy climbed to 1,000 ft and then dived, releasing three 250 lb depth charges which straddled the merchant vessel while his front gunner opened fire. At the same time, the Heinkel reappeared and Cundy turned to attack this aircraft, which took avoiding action. Three more cannon attacks were made on the merchant vessel, interspersed with air combat. The action was eventually broken off owing to shortage of fuel and ammunition.
Ref: AIR 15/263

The merchant vessel was identified as the German *Elsa Essberger* of 6,103 tons. She entered the Spanish port of El Ferrol, and was reported to have suffered damage to her main engines. This photograph was taken on 7 February 1942 from 600 ft by Hudson serial V9092 of 224 Squadron, flown from St Eval by Flt. Lt. Christopher L. Wilson. The crew also photographed Spanish warships and various merchant vessels within the harbour. Photo-interpreters identified a large floating crane alongside the port beam of the German vessel and a dockyard barge by her port bow. She was also riding high, indicating that any leaks had been stopped and that she was carrying little cargo. Repairs seemed to be taking place to her superstructure, probably caused by cannon fire rather than by depth charges.
Ref: AIR 28/733

Three Beauforts of 86 Squadron flew from St Eval in the morning of 17 January 1942 to make an attack on enemy shipping in St Peter Port, Guernsey. Led by Wg. Cdr. Charles J.P. Flood, they attacked in line astern and dropped four 500 lb medium-capacity bombs, two 500 lb general-purpose bombs and twelve 250 lb general-purpose bombs. These sank the French merchant vessel *Ile d'Aix* of 5,028 tons and the German merchant vessel *Madali* of 3,017 tons (although the latter was later refloated), and hit the lighters *Bizerta* and *Diamant* as well as the harbour craft *HS-191* and several cranes. They also machine-gunned German troops. Unfortunately one Guernseyman was killed, as well as several Organisation Todt workers. No Beaufort was hit by the flak defences but one crash-landed at St Mawgan on return, with engine trouble. This photograph shows one of the Beauforts over the port.
Ref: AIR 15/263

Sgt. C.A. Livingstone took off from Wick at 08.28 hours on 8 February 1942 in a Hudson of 608 Squadron, heading for the Norwegian coast. At 11.43 hours the crew spotted an enemy convoy off Lindesnes, consisting of five merchant vessels and one escort vessel. They attacked the rearmost vessel, later estimated at about 1,250 tons, dropping four 250 lb general-purpose bombs from 50 ft. The aircraft was hit in a wing by flak but the crew saw an explosion on the waterline of their target. Nevertheless, there are no German records of any serious damage to a vessel at this time and place.
Ref: AIR 15/263

Wg. Cdr. Charles P.J. Flood led three Beauforts of 86 Squadron on an anti-shipping patrol from St Eval on 16 February 1942. Each aircraft was carrying two 500 lb medium-capacity and two 250 lb general-purpose bombs, all with three seconds delay. In the early afternoon, they came across four small vessels and attacked three of them under the impression that they were enemy coasters. All were sunk, although one lowered a boat and the crew abandoned ship. German records show that they were fishing vessels, the Italian *Balena* of 253 tons, the French *René Cameleyre* of 243 tons, and the French *Jules Pierre* of 231 tons.
Ref: AIR 15/263

At 10.50 hours on 4 May 1942, three Hudsons of 59 Squadron in company with three more from 53 Squadron took off from North Coates to attack an enemy convoy off IJmuiden. They found a convoy of ten vessels and pressed home an attack against the two largest vessels, dropping 100 lb bombs with delay action in the face of very intense flak. Although only near misses were claimed by the crews who returned, three merchant vessels were seriously damaged. These were the Danish *Taarnholm* of 1,420 tons, the German *Janje Fritzen* of 6,582 tons and the Norwegian *Troma* of 5,029 tons. The burst in the background of this photograph, taken from a Hudson of 59 Squadron, is the result of an explosion from a land battery which was also firing at the aircraft. The vessel on the left is the *Janje Fritzen*.
Ref: AIR 15/264

Two Hudsons of 53 Squadron were shot down in this attack. All four men in serial AM530, flown by Sgt. Kenneth M. Nicholls, were killed. The other, serial AM568 flown by Plt. Off. Michael R. Gummer, ditched in the sea and the men clambered onto the wing when their dinghy floated away after inflating, as shown in this photograph. Gummer and one of the WOp/AGs, Sgt. John McCann, were picked up by the Germans and became PoWs, but unhappily the other two men in the crew were drowned. Only a single Hudson of 53 Squadron returned to North Coates from this attack, on one engine. The other engine was smoking and the propeller damaged.
Ref: AIR 28/595

Hudson serial AE642 of 608 Squadron, flown by Fg. Off. Nigel G. Henderson, took off from Wick on 5 May 1942 for the Norwegian coast. The crew sighted a merchant vessel north-west of Haugesund, carrying a deck cargo and escorted by a flak ship. They attacked with four 250 lb bombs. One was a near miss but the others overshot. The Hudson then turned and raked the decks with machine-gun fire. She was the German *Alice Freyman* of 1,377 tons, and the records show that she was badly damaged.
Ref: AIR 15/264

Sunderland serial W3983 of 10 (RAAF) Squadron left Mount Batten at 08.25 hours on 15 May 1942 on a flight to Gibraltar, with Flt. Lt. H.G. Pockley as captain and Plt. Off. A.F. O'Dwyer as 1st pilot. Off Cape Finisterre on the north-west tip of Spain a vessel was picked up on radar at 11.45 hours, from a distance of 20 miles. On approaching, a U-boat was seen submerging alongside a merchant vessel which was armed with a large-calibre gun on the poop and at least two machine-guns on the bridge. A British ensign was seen on the mainmast and a large tricolour roundel on No. 5 hatch. After receiving W/T instructions from base, the Sunderland made seven attacks, releasing eight depth charges in all and exchanging gunfire in which the Sunderland fired 3,500 rounds but received some damage. The flying boat continued shadowing the vessel until fuel shortage forced Pockley to make for Gibraltar, where it moored up at 22.40 hours. The merchant vessel proved to be the German *Munsterland* of 6,408 tons, which was damaged but seen to be unloading at Bordeaux on 19 May.
Ref: AIR 15/264

Right: The Vickers Wellington IC first entered service with Coastal Command in November 1940, when 221 Squadron was formed at Bircham Newton to use the newly developed Air to Surface-Vessel radar. This Wellington IC of 221 Squadron from St Eval was photographed over a German dinghy at 08.30 hours on 23 July 1941 from a Hudson of 233 Squadron after a Focke-Wulf Kondor had been shot down near a convoy west of Northern Ireland. The Leigh Light, designed by Sqn. Ldr. H. de V. 'Sammy' Leigh, was first fitted to a Wellington VIII of 1417 Flight in January 1942. Three months later this Flight became 172 Squadron.
Ref: AIR 27/1438

The first attack with a Leigh Light was made soon after 01.27 hours GMT on 4 June 1942 when Wellington VIII serial ES986 of 172 Squadron, flown by Sqn. Ldr. Jeaffreson H. Greswell from Chivenor in North Devon, lit up a submarine about 70 miles north-west of Cape Peñas on the north coast of Spain. This was the Italian *Luigi Torelli* of 1,036 tons, commanded by Tenente di Vascello (Lieutenant) Augusto Migliorini, which had left La Pallice in the afternoon of 2 June on a war cruise to the West Indies. The Italians did not understand the light and remained on the surface. Greswell dropped four depth charges from 50 ft, straddling the submarine and damaging it so severely that Migliorini was forced to abandon his mission and make for Cape Peñas. At 01.57 hours on his return journey, Greswell attacked a second submarine with machine-gun fire. This was the Italian *Morosini* of 941 tons, which had also left La Pallice for the West Indies and was able to continue. The *Luigi Torelli* ran aground near Cape Peñas but managed to free itself on 6 June. At 07.12 hours on 7 June, it was found near Santander by Sunderland II serial W3994 of 10 (RAAF) Squadron, captained by Plt. Off. T.A. Egerton, from Mount Batten. Egerton dropped a stick of depth charges, as shown in this photograph. The submarine and aircraft exchanged gunfire, during which two members of the Sunderland's crew were injured.
Ref: AIR 27/151

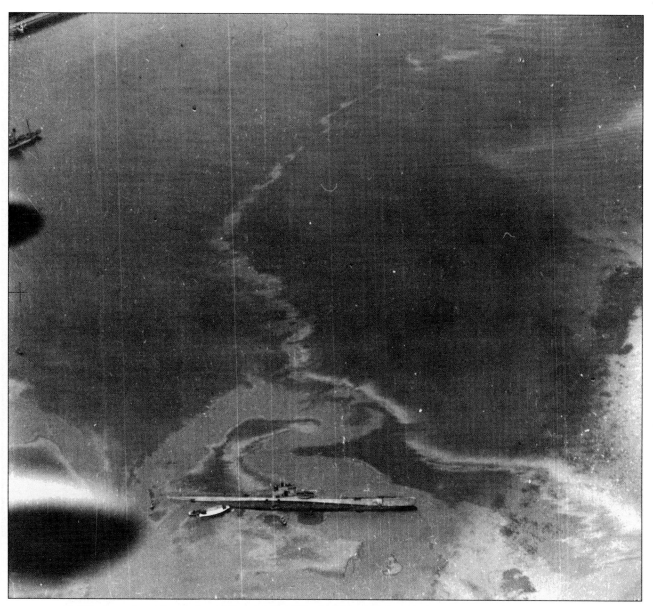

Half an hour later, Sunderland III serial W4019 of 10 (RAAF) Squadron, captained by Flt. Lt. E. St C. Yeoman, arrived on the scene and continued the attack. Although his aircraft was hit in the tail by the Italian submarine, Yeoman released eight depth charges which lifted it upwards by the stern. After exchanging gunfire, Yeoman was forced by shortage of fuel to return to Mount Batten. As a result of the further damage received in these attacks, *Luigi Torelli* put into Santander harbour, where it was beached. It was located at 18.50 hours on 8 June by a Hudson of 53 Squadron, flown by Wg. Cdr. James A. Leggate from St Eval, as shown in this photograph. In danger of internment, it remained there while the crew effected repairs, but put to sea again on 14 June and reached Bordeaux in the late afternoon of the following day. The other submarine attacked on 4 June by the Wellington of 172 Squadron, *Morosini*, completed its mission in the West Indies but was lost from unknown causes while returning to Bordeaux, probably on 10 August 1942.
Ref: AIR 28/733

In the afternoon of 5 June 1942, Sunderland II serial W3986 of 10 (RAAF) Squadron was on patrol from Mount Batten, with Flt. Lt. S.R.C. Wood as captain, when a radar contact was made about 140 miles west of Bordeaux. The Sunderland dived from 5,000 ft to 50 ft and released eight depth charges ahead of a crash-diving U-boat. The U-boat came to the surface and exchanged fire with the Sunderland, as shown in this photograph. The combat lasted about ten minutes, and the Sunderland was hit many times. The U-boat then submerged again. It was the Type VIIC *U-71* which was damaged and forced to return to La Pallice. The Sunderland was later in combat with a Focke-Wulf Kondor. Both aircraft were damaged, and two of the Sunderland crew slightly wounded. The Kondor broke away and the Sunderland returned to base. Wood was awarded a DFC.
Ref: AIR 27/151

An SOS at 03.40 hours on 9 June 1942 from a Halifax of Bomber Command's No. 4 Group alerted the air-sea rescue crews of 279 Squadron. Six Hudsons took off in two waves from Bircham Newton, heading towards the Netherlands. A yellow dinghy was spotted about 60 miles west of The Hague by Plt. Off. D. Boxhall, the air observer in a Hudson flown by Sqn. Ldr. Anthony F. Binks. The crew dropped a Lindholme dinghy (a large central dinghy with four smaller ones roped to it, containing supplies) but this seemed not to inflate properly. A W/T message was sent to Bircham Newton and the other five Hudsons were soon circling the dinghy. At 10.35 hours, RAF High-Speed Launch No. 130 arrived from Yarmouth, and the men were taken to safety.
Ref: AIR 28/77

At 16.10 hours on 23 June 1942, the crew of Whitley VII serial Z9135 of 58 Squadron, flown from St Eval by Flt. Sgt. W. Jones, sighted a surfaced U-boat about 350 miles west of the Gironde estuary. The diving U-boat was straddled from 50 ft with six 250 lb depth charges, four of which were seen to explode on its starboard quarter, leaving a patch of foam and oil. After about five minutes, the bow of the U-boat reappeared and was subjected to fire from the rear turret of the Whitley. The U-boat crew then manned their guns and an exchange of gunfire followed, during which the Whitley was hit in the bomb compartment and upper fuselage but all five gunners on the U-boat were seen to collapse, one falling overboard. The U-boat then submerged, leaving more oil on the surface. It was the Type VIIC *U-753*, which had left La Pallice on 22 April under the command of Kovettenkapitän Alfred Manhardt von Mannstein and was returning from a war cruise in the Caribbean. It was badly damaged but managed to reach La Pallice two days later and underwent extensive repairs.

Ref: AIR 28/733

In April 1942, a crew from 210 Squadron at Sullom Voe in the Shetlands was selected to carry out some special operations over Spitsbergen within the Arctic Circle, the purpose being primarily to carry out reconnaissance over the island. This was associated with a Norwegian expedition to Spitsbergen, partly to deny the use of the territory to the Germans. Two Catalinas were fitted with radar and other instruments, as well as extra fuel tanks which enabled them to stay in the air for over twenty-four hours. Several flights were made, with Flt. Lt. D.E. 'Tim' Healy as captain. At 23.50 hours on 26 June, Catalina serial VA729 flew from Akureyri in Iceland on a photo-reconnaissance sortie of part of the west coast of Spitsbergen. In the morning of 27 June, a Junkers Ju88 was spotted on the German Bansö airstrip south-east of Advent Bay, and the Catalina gunners fired 1,500 rounds at it. The machine was on the strength of Wettererkundungsstaffel 5 at Banak, near the North Cape of Norway, and had been landed there by Leutnant Wagner on 14 June with supplies for German meteorologists, but the propellers had been damaged. It was so badly shot up by the Catalina that it was abandoned.
Ref: AIR 15/470

Unto the Breach
July 1942 – June 1943

By the middle of 1942, Coastal Command was able to face the future with far more confidence. Although there was still a long and bloody war ahead, its aircraft, weaponry and highly-trained aircrews were moving ahead of the enemy's ability to resist its attacks. A role which had been largely defensive had become one of increasing aggression, partly as a result of new tactics but mainly since the strength of the Command was growing steadily.

Ansons had disappeared entirely by this time and only a handful of Blenheims remained. There were still many Hudsons, but most of these aircraft had been transferred to indispensable air-sea rescue duties, a role which they performed admirably. Others were employed on meteorological duties. There were still a few Fleet Air Arm aircraft under Coastal Command control. The new Beaufighter VIC arrived, better armed and more powerful than the Mark IC it replaced. Some of these Beaufighters were being converted to the torpedo role, but Hampdens were still used in this capacity.

The numbers of Wellingtons, Catalinas and Liberators increased to harry the U-boats, all more advanced variants with better detection equipment, although it was not until March 1943 that there were sufficient long-distance aircraft to cover the Atlantic Gap adequately. One squadron was equipped with Fortresses and another with Halifaxes. Whitleys still soldiered on, carrying out useful tasks in the anti-submarine campaign. The numbers of photo-reconnaissance aircraft, mainly Spitfires and Mosquitos, reached a peak which would be sustained until the end of the war. The contribution of these aircraft to British Intelligence was beyond compare. By the end of 1942, the strength of Coastal Command stood at 858 aircraft, and most of these were well equipped and armed.

In the twelve months ending June 1943, there was an enormous increase in the effectiveness of the anti-submarine campaign. Coastal Command sank seventy-one U-boats or Italian submarines and damaged many more, the majority of these in early 1943. Although unable to help close the Atlantic Gap with their shorter range, Leigh Light Wellingtons destroyed so many U-boats in the Bay of Biscay that the head of the Kriegsmarine, Grand Admiral Karl Doenitz, ordered his U-boats to submerge at night during this passage and to surface only by day to recharge batteries. Of course, this practice gave many extra opportunities to the RAF in the Bay of Biscay during daylight hours. Meanwhile, even without the aid of the Wellingtons, sinkings of U-boats in the North Atlantic increased so dramatically that in May 1943 Doenitz decided to order the survivors to move away from the area and operate in the Central Atlantic for the time being.

Similarly, the war against German coastal convoys intensified. The new Beaufighter VIC, carrying bombs but armed with machine-guns and cannons, was the main machine which performed this task in Dutch and German waters, although Hampdens still continued in the torpedo role off the southern coasts of Norway. The numbers of Beaufighters increased enormously, reaching 120 by the end of 1942. This greater strength led to the formation of the first Strike Wing, at North Coates in November 1942. This consisted of only two squadrons at first, and the correct tactics were not devised until the following spring. By this time, a third squadron had been added and the torpedo-carrying variant of the Beaufighter had arrived. Strongly protected by Spitfires of Fighter Command, the North Coates Strike Wing began to sink many ships in German convoys, in spite of increased numbers of flak ships and other escort vessels with heavier armament.

An even deadlier weapon was added to the armoury of the Beaufighters from April 1943: the rocket projectile. Although much practice was needed before the pilots could master the peculiarities of its flight, the rocket projectile fitted with a solid shot warhead would transform the operations of the anti-shipping squadrons and eventually replace the torpedo as the main sinking weapon. On 24 April 1943, a Beaufighter even sank a diving U-boat with four of these projectiles. From this time on, the new Strike Wings of Coastal Command wreaked havoc with the Kriegsmarine along the coasts of occupied Europe.

In the early afternoon of 17 July 1942, the Type VIIC *U-751*, commanded by Korvettenkapitän Gerhard Bigalk, was on the surface about 450 miles out in the North Atlantic from St Nazaire when it was attacked by a Whitley of 502 Squadron flown from St Eval by Plt. Off. A.R.A. Hunt. Depth charges and anti-submarine bombs were dropped and the Whitley then made several machine-gun attacks. The U-boat slid under the sea stern first. About an hour later, Lancaster serial R5724 of 61 Squadron also arrived, flown by Flt. Lt. Peter R. Casement. This was one of several Lancasters of 61 Squadron on detachment from Bomber Command to Coastal Command at St Eval for a short experimental period. The crew of the Lancaster saw an oil slick and then the U-boat, which had resurfaced and was obviously in difficulties. Casement made two attacks with depth charges and anti-submarine bombs while his gunners picked off seamen trying to man their guns. The U-boat sank while several of the crew abandoned ship. It was on its seventh war cruise.
Ref: AIR 28/733

Sunderland serial W4004 of 10 (RAAF) Squadron left Mount Batten at 01.20 hours on 26 July 1942, captained by Flt. Lt. D. Vernon with Fg. Off. K.C. Beeton as 1st pilot, on a patrol over the Bay of Biscay. At 06.24 hours, while about 15 miles north-east of Bilbao on the north coast of Spain, the crew homed on to a merchant vessel and two trawlers with their Air to Surface-Vessel radar. This area had been designated 'free-for-all' by the Allies, since blockade runners were carrying essential war supplies such as wolfram from German mines in Spain to Bordeaux. After reporting by W/T to base, Vernon attacked at 07.00 hours, diving from cloud at 2,000 ft and dropping two 250 lb anti-submarine bombs from 1,000 ft. On the run-up, the trawlers opened up with medium and heavy flak, while the merchant vessel fired with cannons. The Sunderland replied with all guns, concentrating on the bridge of the merchant vessel, which was flying the Spanish flag. After pulling up into cloud, the Sunderland made a second machine-gun attack, being met with heavy return fire from the trawlers, although the merchant vessel was silenced. A third attack was made, once more with machine-guns, but two Torpex depth charges were dropped on this occasion. The trawlers continued to fire at the Sunderland. Smoke from explosions was seen to be streaming from the superstructure of the merchant vessel, which headed for the Spanish coast at a much reduced speed, accompanied by the trawlers. She was later identified as the Spanish *Castilio Almansa* of 1,407 tons. The Sunderland resumed patrol and was waterborne at 12.35 hours.
Ref: AIR 15/265

At 10.30 hours on 1 September 1942 the Italian submarine *Reginaldo Guiliani* of 1,031 tons was returning from a successful war cruise in the West Indies, in which it had sunk four Allied merchant vessels, when it was attacked by two Sunderlands of 10 (RAAF) Squadron from Mount Batten. The attack took place while it was on the surface recharging batteries about 200 miles west of the submarine's base of La Pallice. The first Sunderland, serial W3986 captained by Flt. Lt. S.R.C. Wood, dived down under fire from the submarine and released four 250 lb semi-armour piercing bombs. The second Sunderland, serial W3983 captained by Flt. Lt. H.G. Pockley, attacked with two 250 lb bombs. Pockley then made another attack, releasing a single bomb, but his aircraft was hit by return fire. The bombs caused no serious damage, but the commander, Capitano di Fregata (Captain) Giovanni Bruno, was seriously wounded in the throat by gunfire and handed over to his first officer, Tenente di Vascello (Lieutenant) Ariedo Calzigna. A third Sunderland, serial T9085 of 461 (RAAF) Squadron captained by Plt. Off. B.L. Buls, also arrived from Mount Batten, and the three captains discussed a concerted attack on their R/Ts. Fortunately for the Italians, all aircraft were ordered by Mount Batten to discontinue the attack and hunt their primary target with their remaining bombs, although this was not found. This photograph was taken from Flt. Lt. Pockley's Sunderland.
Ref: AIR 27/151

The submarine made for Santander in Spain with the wounded, but was spotted at 11.40 hours the following day about 80 miles north-west of this port by the crew of Wellington IC serial HF894 of 304 (Polish) Squadron, flown from Dale in Pembrokeshire by Fg. Off. M. Kucharski. Six depth charges were dropped. One hit the deck and rolled into the sea while the others fell close to the hull, exploding and seriously damaging the double hull, as well as blowing two seamen into the water and wounding others. Kucharski made two more attacks with two 250 lb bombs, but these missed narrowly. Five machine-gun attacks followed, wounding more seamen. The Wellington returned to base at 12.30 hours.
Ref: AIR 15/470

The enforced return of the Wellington was a godsend for the damaged *Reginaldo Guiliani*, for it was without light, in danger of sinking and unable to return fire. However, it managed to limp into Santander the following morning, where the wounded were put ashore and repairs continued. Spitfire PR D serial BR420 of No. 1 Photo-Reconnaissance Unit, flown from St Eval on 4 September by Fg. Off. R.P. Johnson, brought back this photograph of the submarine listing to port and down at the stern. It remained at Santander until 8 November 1942, when it was able to put to sea again, although only on the surface. Escorted by relays of German aircraft, it arrived the next day at Le Verdon, near Bordeaux.
Ref: AIR 15/470

The Coastal Command station of North Front in Gibraltar was the main airfield for land-based aircraft during the Anglo-American landings in French North Africa, which began on 8 November 1942 under the code-name of Operation Torch. The runway was widened beforehand and extended 450 yd into the sea, to accommodate the huge air effort. In the first week of the invasion, aircraft were landing or taking off from North Front at the rate of over one every eight minutes.
Ref: AIR 15/470

This Whitley VII serial Z9199 of 502 Squadron, flown from St Eval at 05.00 hours on 16 November 1942 by Plt. Off. W.S. Biggar, came down in the sea at 12.20 hours about 300 miles west of Lorient while returning to base with engine trouble. Fortunately it was seen by another Whitley of 502 Squadron, flown by Fg. Off. S.A. Fox, and photographed while the crew were launching two dinghies. The second Whitley remained on station as long as possible and an air-sea rescue Hudson dropped a Lindholme dinghy. The six men were picked up by a Polish destroyer the following day. Ref: AIR 28/733

Early versions of the Bristol Beaufighter proved remarkably successful as powerfully armed and robust long-distance fighters in Coastal Command. Trials were carried out from July 1942 on a Beaufighter VI by the Torpedo Development Unit at Gosport in Hampshire, using a variant of the Mark XII 18-in torpedo which could be dropped from higher speeds. These proved successful and the outcome was a version known as the Torbeau. One result was the formation of the North Coates Strike Wing in November 1942, consisting of 254 Squadron armed with torpedoes and cannons and 236 Squadron armed with cannons, machine-guns and bombs. This photograph was taken at the Torpedo Development Unit.
Ref: AVIA 16/67

The first attack made by the newly formed North Coates Strike Wing was not a success. Twenty-six Beaufighters took off at about 15.15 hours on 20 November 1942, comprising fourteen Mark VICs of 236 Squadron led by Wg. Cdr. H.D. Fraser for anti-flak and bombing, with twelve of 254 Squadron led by Wg. Cdr. R.E.X. Mack. Ten of those in 254 Squadron carried torpedoes while two were in the anti-flak role. Spitfire escorts from Coltishall in Norfolk missed the rendezvous and the formation headed for the Hook of Holland without them. They found two heavily armed and escorted convoys and attacked both. There was heavy flak followed by attacks from Focke-Wulf FW190 fighters from Schipol.
Ref: AIR 15/470

The Beaufighter crews attacked with great determination, but not in a coordinated manner. Three aircraft were shot down and their crews killed, two crashed on return and five more were badly damaged. The main vessel in the German convoy approaching Rotterdam, *Schiff 49* (formerly the Dutch *Amerskerk*) of 7,900 tons, was only slightly damaged, as were two of the escort vessels. The only vessel sunk was the naval tug *BS4* (formerly the Dutch *Indus*) of 449 tons.
Ref: AIR 28/595

The Handley Page Halifax II began to enter service with Coastal Command at the end of 1942, being known as the GR II. The machines were fitted with Air to Surface-Vessel radar and employed mainly on anti-submarine and meteorological duties, but later versions additionally carried out bombing attacks

against enemy ports. This example of a Halifax underwent tactical trials at the Air Fighting Development Unit in June 1941.
Ref: AIR 16/933

In April 1944, the Coastal Command Development Unit attempted to fit a Leigh Light (code-named 'Pumpkin A') in the bomb bay of a Halifax. However, the installation proved unsatisfactory since the bay and its door cut off part of the beam when the light was depressed by means of a Bowden cable. Nose and wing installations also proved so discouraging that all attempts were abandoned. It was also considered not worthwhile to try the light on a Sunderland. However, the Leigh Light already performed magnificently on the Wellington and the Liberator. It was responsible for illuminating numerous submarines at night, when they rose to the surface to run at speed and recharge their batteries. These were first detected by Air to Surface-Vessel radar and many surprise attacks were achieved, often resulting in sinkings. The Leigh Light was hated by the German U-boat crews, who referred to it as 'das verdammte Licht' – that damned light.

Ref: AIR 65/94

In May 1941, surviving Boeing Fortress Is of Bomber Command were transferred to Coastal Command for use in maritime reconnaissance. These were adapted from the B-17C Flying Fortress, and later versions adapted from the B-17E and the B 17F were known as Fortress IIs and IIIs. This Fortress I serial AN537 of 220 Squadron based in Northern Ireland, was photographed over an Atlantic convoy. Ref: AIR 15/470

At 12.22 hours on 27 February 1943, Sqn. Ldr. P.G. Evans took off from St Eval in Fortress IIA serial FL462 of 59 Squadron on a special anti-shipping patrol heading for the Azores. The aircraft and crew were on detachment from their base at Chivenor in North Devon. At 16.55 hours a Focke-Wulf Kondor was spotted and attacked. Although hits were scored, Evans broke away in order to carry out his primary task. When about 400 miles from the Azores, he sighted his objective, a burning enemy vessel. This was the German prize tanker *Hohenfriedburg*, formerly the Norwegian *Herborg* of 7,892 tons. While being escorted home during the previous morning by the U-boats *U-264*, *U-258* and *U-437*, she had been spotted and reported by a Liberator of the USAAF. The U-boats were part of the *Rochen* Group, operating north of the Azores, but cruisers of the Home Fleet were also in the area and HMS *Sussex* closed with the tanker and shelled her. Aware of the presence of U-boats, the cruiser did not stop to pick up survivors and in fact avoided four torpedoes fired by *U-264*. The Fortress crew saw that the tanker was burning and sinking, with four lifeboats to her north. They returned to St Eval and landed at 01.25 hours the following morning.
Ref: AIR 28/741

At 15.03 hours on 22 March 1943, the crew of Whitley V serial Z6950 of No. 10 Operational Training Unit (OTU), flown from St Eval by Sgt. J.A. Marsden, spotted a U-boat on the surface about 300 miles west of St Nazaire. The Whitley was being flown at 100 ft in poor visibility, and Marsden immediately turned to port and released six depth charges which straddled the U-boat, although no results could be seen. The U-boat was the Type VIIC *U-665*, commanded by Oberleutnant zur See Hans-Jürgen Haupt, which had left Kiel on 20 February on its maiden war cruise and was heading for a French port. It was sunk with all hands. No. 10 OTU was on detachment from Bomber Command, having arrived at St Eval on 1 August 1942. The crews and their instructors spent the last three weeks of their course on anti-submarine sorties over the Bay of Biscay, under Coastal Command control.
Ref: AIR 28/741

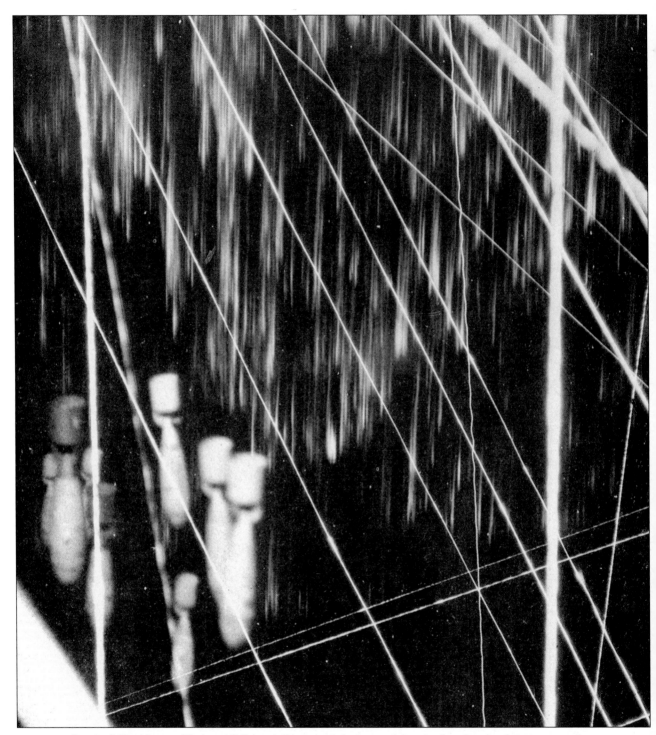

Bombs falling from a Hudson of Coastal Command during a night attack at low level on a port, taken by 320 (Dutch) or 407 (RCAF) Squadron in early 1943. Tracks of searchlights, flak and tracer provide the only illumination during the film exposure.
Ref: AIR 15/470

Handley Page Hampden Is were handed over to Coastal Command when they became obsolescent with Bomber Command in early 1942. This example, serial P5338, was tested successfully as a torpedo-bomber by the Torpedo Development Unit at Gosport during February 1942. In April, Bomber Command transferred 144 Squadron and 455 (RAAF) Squadron to Coastal Command. These converted to torpedo work, and Coastal Command's 415 (RCAF) and 489 (RNZAF) Squadrons also received these machines. Their use was only temporary, pending the arrival of Beaufighter torpedo-bombers from November 1942.
Ref: AVIA 16/62

Three Hampdens of 489 (RNZAF) Squadron took off from Wick at 07.32 hours on 4 April 1943 to patrol the Norwegian coast, flown by Fg. Off. S. Letta, Warr. Off. R.C. Dunn and Warr. Off. J. Dubbury. They came across a merchant vessel escorted by a flak ship off Kristiansand North and approached low over the water, inshore of the target. Complete surprise was achieved and torpedoes were released from 600 yd before the flak ship opened fire. Letta's torpedo was photographed exploding against the vessel, which listed to starboard and turned for shore. All the aircraft returned safely. The vessel was the German troop carrier *Altair* of 6,800 tons, which sank before reaching shore.
Ref: AIR 15/470

The second attack made by the North Coates Strike Wing was an unqualified success. The Wing had been joined by the Beaufighters of 143 Squadron. Coordinated tactics had been worked out by the commanding officer of 236 Squadron, Wg. Cdr. H. Neil G. Wheeler, who also insisted on strong fighter cover. Led by Wheeler, twenty-one Beaufighters of the three squadrons took off soon after 13.15 hours on 18 April 1943, escorted by twenty-two long-range Spitfires of 118 and 167 Squadrons from Coltishall, as well as eight Mustangs of 613 Squadron. The whole formation reached a large German convoy off the Dutch island of Texel. This photograph, taken from a Beaufighter of 143 Squadron, shows an M-class minesweeper escort under cannon fire by an anti-flak Beaufighter.
Ref: AIR 28/595

The German convoy consisted of eight merchant ships escorted by eight heavily armed minesweepers and flak ships, heading north. The Beaufighters attacked against intense light and heavy flak. The main target, the Dutch merchant vessel *Hoegh Carrier* of 4,906 tons, was torpedoed and sunk, while four of the escort vessels were badly damaged. Every RAF aircraft returned. This attack marked the turning point of Coastal Command's efforts to obliterate Germany's vital coastal trade with Sweden, consisting mainly of coal heading north and high-quality iron ore heading south.
Ref: AIR 15/470

Another attack by the North Coates Strike Wing, led by Wg. Cdr. H. Neil G. Wheeler in the late afternoon of 29 April 1943, yielded impressive results. Twenty-seven Beaufighters of 143, 236 and 254 Squadrons took off, escorted by twenty-four Spitfires of 118 and 167 Squadrons together with six Mustangs of 613 Squadron. They attacked an enemy convoy off Texel, consisting of six merchant vessels flying balloons, escorted by nine flak ships and minesweepers. The Dutch merchant vessel *Alundra* of 4,930 tons, the Swedish merchant vessel *Narvik* of 4,251 tons and the German flak ship *Auguste Kampf* of 385 tons were all sunk. One Beaufighter of 143 Squadron was shot down and the crew lost their lives.
Ref: AIR 28/595

The next attack by the North Coates Strike Wing took place on 17 May 1943, once again led by Wg. Cdr. H. Neil G. Wheeler. A north-bound convoy was known to have left Rotterdam, consisting of six merchant vessels flying balloons escorted by seven minesweepers or flak ships. Twenty-seven Beaufighters took off in mid-afternoon, escorted by fifty-nine Spitfires of 118, 167, 302, 308 and 402 Squadrons of Fighter Command's No. 12 Group. They caught up with the convoy off Texel and sank the German merchant vessel *Kyphyssia* of 2,964 tons, the M-class minesweeper *M.414* of 750 tons and the flak ship *Hermann Hindrichs* of 523 tons, in addition to damaging other vessels. All the RAF aircraft returned safely.
Ref: AIR 28/595

Another attack by the North Coates Strike Wing, led by Wg. Cdr. H. Neil G. Wheeler on 24 May 1943, did not achieve the expected results. There was no precise knowledge of the position of the enemy and the weather was poor. At one time, some fishing vessels were mistaken for the convoy and the aircraft became dispersed. An attack against a convoy took place eventually, as shown in this photograph of the German *Stadt Emden* of 5,180 tons, but there were no sinkings. All aircraft returned safely.
Ref: AIR 28/595

On 8 June 1943 a Hudson III of 269 Squadron flown from Reykjavik by Sgt R.B. Couchman came across a U-boat near a convoy about 250 miles south of Iceland. Couchman dived from 2,500 ft and straddled the U-boat with four depth charges, being met with intense flak. The U-boat circled, trailing oil, and submerged. It was the Type IXC *U-535* commanded by Kapitänleutnant Helmut Ellmenreich, returning from its first war cruise, from Kiel to the Azores. Ellmenreich made for France but before reaching safety his unlucky *U-535* was sunk on 5 July by an attack made by Liberator GR V serial BZ751 of 53 Squadron, flown from St Eval by Flt. Sgt. W. Anderson.
Ref: AIR 27/1568

On 13 June 1943, Wg. Cdr. H. Neil G. Wheeler led the North Coates Strike Wing against a north-bound convoy off Den Helder, consisting of three merchant vessels and seven escorts. The aircraft met tremendous flak. One of the Beaufighters of 143 Squadron was shot down and the men were killed. However, the largest ship in the convoy, the German *Stadt Emden* of 5,180 tons which had escaped damage during the attack of 24 May 1943, was torpedoed and sunk. A flak ship, *Vp 1109* of 487 tons, was also sunk.
Ref: AIR 28/595

The first rocket attack by Beaufighters of the North Coates Strike Wing against an enemy convoy took place on 22 June 1943, led by Wg. Cdr. H. Neil G. Wheeler. There were thirty-six Beaufighters in all, twenty of which were armed with rockets fitted with 60 lb solid-shot warheads, intended to be aimed so as to penetrate below the waterline. They were escorted by three squadrons of Spitfires and two of Typhoons. Their target was a south-bound convoy consisting of five Swedish merchant vessels, heavily escorted by no fewer than fifteen minesweepers or flak ships. By this time, the Germans had added 'parachute and cable' rockets and even flame-throwers to their defences. The formation attacked the target off Scheveningen and achieved surprise, seriously damaging three flak ships.
Ref: AIR 28/595

During the attack of 22 June 1943, the Torbeau crews of 254 Squadron had been briefed to attack slightly later than usual, to avoid being hit by the new rockets. They received the full force of the defences, while the vessels had time to turn and avoid their torpedoes. Two of these torpedo-bombers were shot down and their crews killed, and three more crash-landed back in England. This photograph, taken by the navigator of one of the Torbeaus, shows another crashing near the convoy.
Ref: AIR 28/595

The next attack with rockets was made by the North Coates Strike Wing on 27 June 1943, led by the 'Wing Commander Flying' at the station, Wg. Cdr. W.A.L. 'Wally' Davis. On this occasion, twenty-one aircraft from 143 and 236 Squadrons took off, all armed with rockets, but the Torbeaus of 254 Squadron did not participate. The formation attacked a south-bound convoy off The Hague, consisting of four merchant vessels escorted by eleven flak ships and minesweepers. No surprise was achieved and the defenders put up an enormous wall of flak. Nevertheless, all the Beaufighters returned safely, but without scoring any successes. The techniques of firing rockets had not been fully mastered, although these weapons were to become the most effective in the armoury of the Strike Wings.
Ref: AIR 28/595

THE BLAST OF WAR
JULY 1943 – JUNE 1944

By July 1943, Coastal Command was in good shape, with up-to-date aircraft and squadrons which were carrying out their tasks efficiently and successfully. The aircrews and ground staff of the Command were in good heart, knowing that their efforts were making a vital contribution to the ultimate victory which was confidently expected. At this time, North Africa was in Allied hands, Italy was reeling and approaching capitulation, the Japanese were falling back in the Pacific and South-East Asia, and the Germans were in retreat in Russia. An invasion in the West was expected, with only the timing in doubt. However, the Germans were fighting stubbornly and their resources were still huge. It was dangerous to underestimate them.

The anti-submarine squadrons of Coastal Command continued to receive new aircraft, with many of the squadrons converting to longer-range aircraft. By the end of 1943, there were 105 Liberators in the Command, which also controlled 36 Liberators of the USAAF and USNAF. After negotiations with the Portuguese, the RAF was allowed to use the Azores from late 1943, so that this base as well as Iceland enabled aircraft to cover the former Atlantic Gap. The numbers of Catalinas, Sunderlands, Fortresses, Halifaxes and Wellingtons remained fairly static, but those of Hudsons were declining. In early 1944 all the remaining Whitleys were phased out. In the anti-shipping squadrons, the number of Beaufighters increased to 167 by the end of 1943. The Hampdens had also been phased out and

replaced by Beaufighters. The photo-reconnaissance aircraft became more numerous, as did the meteorological aircraft. By 1 January 1944, the Command was equipped with 889 aircraft, almost exactly five times its strength at the beginning of the war. Moreover, almost all these were modern aircraft fitted with advanced equipment.

The Germans were not idle in their efforts to minimize the sinkings of their U-boats by Coastal Command. An experimental U-boat was heavily armed and invited attack by remaining on the surface in the Bay of Biscay. Unfortunately for the project, this vessel was discovered by three Beaufighters, which killed ten of the crew and wounded thirteen others in the ensuing air/sea combat. Another tactic, grouping together for common defence, merely resulted in mass attacks from aircraft. New devices were devised to counter the RAF's radar, but the British scientists also moved ahead. The most effective of the German inventions was the Schnorkel, a breathing tube which enabled the U-boat to remain under water for very long periods, but only a few new U-boats were fitted with this device before D-Day.

In the twelve months leading up to June 1944, Coastal Command sank no fewer than 114 U-boats and damaged many more. The course of the war at sea had been completely altered. In the earlier part of the war, Britain had been at severe risk from the rate of merchant vessels sunk by U-boats. When its losses from Coastal Command activities were added to those from other causes such as sinkings by the

Royal Navy, the Kriegsmarine was experiencing a rate of loss which it could not sustain, either in replacement vessels or newly trained crews.

Meanwhile, the activities of the anti-shipping squadrons intensified. The creation of the North Coates Strike Wing was followed by three others equipped with Beaufighters. All these were supplied with the new Beaufighter TFX, fitted with even more powerful engines and an extended fin which gave greater stability at low level. It could be used for anti-flak or as a torpedo carrier, but the rocket projectile was replacing the torpedo as the main sinking weapon. The Wick Strike Wing was formed in October 1943 and the Leuchars Strike Wing in March 1944. The Davidstow Strike Wing, covering the west coast of France, was formed in May 1944. This was joined by another in June 1944, the Portreath Strike Wing equipped with Mosquito VIs and XVIIIs. The Mosquito entered Coastal Command as a strike aircraft in October 1943 but at first the

squadrons did not form part of a Strike Wing. There was always friendly rivalry between the Beaufighter and Mosquito squadrons about the respective merits of their aircraft, both having their devotees. Both types of aircraft were responsible for numerous sinkings of enemy vessels, on a scale which increased steadily until the end of the war.

When the great enterprise of the invasion began on 6 June 1944, the task of the Coastal Command squadrons based in England and Wales was to help guard the flanks of the seaborne force as it sailed from Littlehampton to the beaches of Normandy, and then to ensure that a stream of supplies was unmolested. Enemy forces, such as U-boats and destroyers based in French ports and E-boats from the east, attempted to interfere with the Allied force, but the combined protection of the Royal Navy and Coastal Command ensured that most of these were sunk and the remainder repelled.

A Liberator I serial AM929 which first entered service with 120 Squadron at Ballykelly on 1 August 1942 and subsequently had an adventurous career.
Ref: AIR 15/472

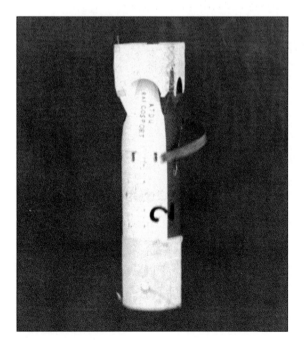

The acoustic homing torpedo, known by the cover name 'Mark 24 Mine' was developed by US scientists and first arrived in Britain in April 1943. It was first carried by the Liberators of 120 Squadron in the following month but remained a highly secret weapon throughout the war, being used by the RAF on Liberator squadrons operating in mid-Atlantic.
Ref: CN 1/5

At 18.03 hours on 24 July 1943, a Liberator V of 224 Squadron from St Eval was on an anti-submarine patrol in the Bay of Biscay when a dinghy containing five occupants was spotted about 75 miles north of El Ferrol on the north-west tip of Spain. The men were obviously Germans, wearing khaki uniform. The Liberator was flown by Sqn. Ldr. Terence M. Bulloch, who spent eight minutes over the dinghy and dropped two emergency packs, one of which fell very close to it. Bulloch was one of the most successful anti-submarine pilots in Coastal Command during the Second World War.
Ref: AIR 28/741

The US Eighth Air Force despatched 264 B-17 Flying Fortresses on a daylight raid to Hamburg on 25 July 1943, in between Bomber Command's massive night raids on the city. Nineteen of these Fortresses failed to return but some ditched in the North Sea. The ten-man crew of this Fortress had difficulty getting into their dinghies but an airborne lifeboat was dropped by one of Coastal Command's Hudsons, which by this stage in the war were primarily engaged on air-sea rescue duties. The crew clambered into the lifeboat, started up the engine and set course for the English coast. They were met by the RAF's High-Speed Launch No. 2551 and taken into Yarmouth.
Ref: AIR 15/471

On 28 July 1943, two Beaufighter XICs of 404 (RCAF) Squadron took off from Sumburgh in the Shetlands to act as screens for the cruiser HMS *Belfast* and four destroyers to the north-east. The aircraft were directed by the naval force to enemy aircraft which could be detected on radar. The pilot of one Beaufighter, Fg. Off. Sydney S. Shulemson, encountered a Bloem & Voss BV138 tri-motored flying boat which was shadowing the British warships, and shot it down into the sea, as shown in this photograph. One survivor scrambled out of the top hatch and Shulemson asked HMS *Belfast* to rescue him, but by the time a destroyer arrived the man had disappeared. Shortly afterwards the second Beaufighter, flown by Sqn. Ldr. Al De la Haye, pursued and shot down another BV138. On this occasion the flying boat crashed into the sea and broke up, with no hope of survivors.
Ref: AIR 15/471

A successful attack was made by the North Coates Strike Wing on 2 August 1943, led by Wg. Cdr. H. Neil G. Wheeler. Thirty-six Beaufighters of 143, 236 and 254 Squadrons, escorted by fifty-one Spitfire Vs of 118, 402 (RCAF), 416 (RCAF) and 611 Squadrons, attacked a large south-bound convoy off the Dutch island of Texel, consisting of six merchant vessels carrying iron ore, escorted by no fewer than four minesweepers and ten flak ships. The anti-flak Beaufighters, some of which were carrying rockets, seriously damaged seven flak ships, while torpedoes of 254 Squadron sank the merchant vessel *Fortuna* of 2,700 tons and the flak ship *Vp1108* of 314 tons. The Spitfires shot down two of four defending Messerschmitt Bf109s. The attackers suffered no losses, although some were hit, while the shattered convoy turned into Den Helder with numerous dead and wounded.
Ref: AIR 28/595

The Type VIIC U-boat *U-617*, commanded by Kapitänleutnant Albrecht Brandi, was beached near Cape Tres Porcas on the coast of Spanish Morocco after being attacked in the early hours of 12 September 1943 by two Leigh Light Wellingtons of 179 Squadron from North Front in Gibraltar. The first, flown by Sqn. Ldr. D.B. Hodgkinson of the RCAF, straddled the U-boat with a stick of six depth charges. The second, flown by Plt. Off. W.H. Brunini, attacked two hours later with six more depth charges in the face of accurate flak which killed the rear gunner, Sgt. W. Jones of the RAAF. Later in the morning, the beached U-boat was attacked with bombs and rockets by Hudsons of 48 and 233 Squadrons from Gibraltar, although by this time the crew appeared to have got ashore. It was also attacked by Swordfish of the Fleet Air Arm and shelled by units of the Royal Navy. The destruction of the U-boat raised the question of whether Spanish neutrality had been infringed or whether the doctrine of 'hot pursuit' held good. This photograph was taken from a Hudson of 48 Squadron flown by the commanding officer, Wg. Cdr. T.F.U. Lang. The Hudson was fired at from the shore but did not retaliate.
Ref: AIR 27/472

The abandoned *U-617* after the Royal Navy had made certain that it would never put to sea again.
Ref: AIR 15/471

On 16 September 1943, twelve Beaufighters of 236 Squadron and eleven of 254 Squadron from the North Coates Strike Wing, led by Wg. Cdr. W.A.L. 'Wally' Davis, attacked a convoy of six M-class minesweepers and two trawlers off Den Helder. The Beaufighters were armed with cannons or rockets and escorted by two squadrons of Spitfires. The vessels were raked with cannon fire and hit with rockets, as shown in this photograph, but there were no sinkings, according to German records. The enemy vessels responded with very intense light flak and four Messerschmitt Bf109s attempted to interfere with the operation. Two Beaufighters of 236 Squadron did not return, lost from unknown causes, and four other aircraft were damaged.
Ref: AIR 28/595

The North Coates Strike Wing made another attack on 25 September 1943, when Wg. Cdr. W.A.L. 'Wally' Davis led eleven Beaufighters of 236 Squadron and thirteen of 254 Squadron to a convoy of four merchant vessels and about fourteen escorts off Den Helder, all flying balloons. The formation was escorted by Spitfires and on this occasion five of 254 Squadron's aircraft carried torpedoes. Many hits were scored on the escort vessels with cannons and all the torpedoes were dropped, but the flak was extremely intense and two Beaufighters were shot down, including one flown by the commanding officer of 254 Squadron. One enemy vessel was sunk in the attack, the flak ship *Vp316* of 550 tons.
Ref: AIR 28/595

In the morning of 8 October 1943, two U-boats were sunk by Coastal Command while escorting the same convoy about 450 miles south of Reykjavik. The first was attacked at 08.56 hours by Liberator III serial FL930 of 86 Squadron, flown from Ballykelly in Londonderry by Flt. Lt. J. Wright, who dropped a stick of four depth charges over a diving U-boat without apparent result. The same U-boat was sighted at 09.54 hours and two more depth charges were dropped, which caused a violent explosion. The bows of the U-boat were seen sticking up from the sea, with men in the water, before it sank. It was the Type VIIC *U-419* from Bergen, commanded by Oberleutnant zur See Dietrich Giersburg, who was the only man the escort vessels were able to rescue. Another U-boat was sighted at 11.10 hours and attacked with machine-gun fire, but soon afterwards Liberator GRV serial FL965 of 86 Squadron, flown by Fg. Off. C.W. Burcher, arrived and took up the attack. He dropped four depth charges at 11.40 hours, which seemed to cause some damage, and then Liberator III serial FK233 of 120 Squadron, flown from Reykjavik by Fg. Off. D.C.L. Webber, also arrived. At 12.13 hours, Webber dropped four depth charges on the U-boat, which was again submerging. Both Burcher and Webber dropped two more depth charges apiece and then made several machine-gun attacks. The crew began to stream out of the conning tower, as shown in this photograph. It was the Type VIIC *U-643* from Bergen, commanded by Kapitänleutnant Hans Harold Speidel, and it exploded and sank at 14.45 hours. Twenty-one of the crew were rescued by British destroyers.
Ref: AIR 15/471

On 19 October 1943, the North Coates Strike Wing sent out fifteen Beaufighters of 254 Squadron and twelve of 236 Squadron on a Rover patrol off the area of IJmuiden, escorted by Spitfires. The formation, led by Sqn. Ldr. William D.L. Filson-Young of 254 Squadron, encountered the German liner *Strassburg* of 17,001 tons, which had been stranded since 3 September. A flak ship and an armed tug were in attendance, probably trying to salvage the liner. The Beaufighters attacked with rockets and cannons, raking all vessels and setting the liner and the tug on fire. They met concentrated flak from the shore as well as the vessels, and one Beaufighter failed to return.
Ref: AIR 28/595

In the morning of 22 November 1943, Sub-Lt. Finn Eriksrud took off from Leuchars in a Mosquito FBVI of 333 (Norwegian) Squadron on a patrol from Stavanger to Lister. At 10.08 hours a Junkers Ju88 was sighted about 1,000 yd away, the German crew not seeming to realize that an RAF aircraft was approaching. Eriksrud closed to 600 yd from dead astern, at a height of 200 ft, and opened fire. Pieces of the fuselage fell off the enemy aircraft and its starboard engine caught fire. It dived into the sea and disappeared. German records show that it was a Ju88D-1, radio code D7+BH, of *Westa 1*, which had taken off from Zwischenhahn in north Germany on a weather reconnaissance over the North Sea. On the return journey, it was diverted to Stavanger owing to deteriorating weather conditions in Germany. All four crew members were killed. Eriksrud and his navigator Erling V. Johannsen made a forced landing at Bömlo in Norway on 18 December 1943, after another combat, and spent the rest of the war as PoWs.
Ref: AIR 15/471

The Italian merchant vessel *Pietro Orseolo* of 6,344 tons was employed by the Axis as a blockade runner between France and the Far East. She left Kobe on 25 January 1943 with ninety passengers, mainly German military personnel who were being repatriated, and then picked up a cargo of 5,500 tons of natural rubber from Singapore. After another stop in Djakarta she headed on 16 February for France. On the last lap of her journey, while being escorted by four German destroyers in the Bay of Biscay, she was hit by a torpedo fired by the USS *Shad* but did not sink and entered Le Verdon on 1 April. Italy surrendered to the Allies on 7 September 1943 and control of the ship was taken over by the Germans. She was sent to deep water anchorage off Port-Tudy in the Ile de Groix, where she was spotted on 26 November by an RAF photo-reconnaissance aircraft. On the following day, she was bombed by three Mosquito VIs of 487 (RNZAF) Squadron, part of the 2nd Tactical Air Force, escorted by twelve Typhoons, but suffered only superficial damage. She was then moved to an alternative anchorage off Concarneau, where she joined another blockade runner and was protected by six M-class minesweepers. Eventually located again by the RAF, the blockade runner was attacked once more, on 18 December 1943, by six torpedo-carrying Beaufighters of 254 Squadron detached from North Coates to Predannack in Cornwall, with six anti-flak Beaufighters of 248 Squadron. They were escorted by eight Typhoons, and the formation was led by Wg. Cdr. A.W. Darley Miller. The attack was made in the face of intense flak, but the *Pietro Orseolo* was hit amidships by two torpedoes, as shown in this photograph, and some of the escort vessels were damaged. Some of the aircraft were hit but all returned. The blockade runner remained afloat but exploded and sank the following morning while under tow. Ref: AIR 15/471

Lagens airfield in the Azores, photographed on 2 September 1944 from 5,000 ft by a Fortress of 220 Squadron, which was based there from October 1943 after the Portuguese granted facilities to the

Allies. Two new runways were still under construction.
Ref: AIR 15/472

At 11.54 hours on 8 January 1944, Sunderland III serial EK586 of 10 (RAAF) Squadron from Mount Batten was on patrol about 400 miles west of St Nazaire when a U-boat was spotted about 12 miles away. The aircraft was captained by Fg. Off. J.P. Roberts, with Flt. Lt. S.W. Ashdown as 1st pilot. An attack was made four minutes later, opening fire from the front turret in the face of return fire, but the depth charge system did not function and the attack was aborted. Six depth charges were dropped on a second run, straddling the stern of the U-boat and exploding. Sailors climbed out of the conning tower while the bows rose and there was an explosion, leaving many of the crew in the sea. It was learned that this was the Type VIIC *U-426*, commanded by Kapitänleutnant Christian Reich, which had left Brest five days earlier for the North Atlantic. There were no survivors from the crew. This photograph shows the U-boat under machine-gun attack before finally sinking.
Ref: AIR 27/153

The Type VIIC U-boat *U-571*, commanded by Oberleutnant zur See Gustav Lüssow, was attacked on 28 January 1944 about 200 miles west of the Shannon estuary by Sunderland serial EK577 of 461 (RAAF) Squadron flown from Pembroke Dock by Flt. Lt. R.D. Lucas. The target was picked up in poor weather. Lucas attacked with four depth charges, which fell short. The U-boat fired at the Sunderland but the gunners were put out of action by return fire. Lucas attacked again, with two depth charges which straddled the conning tower. The U-boat blew up, shown faintly below the nose of the float in this photograph, leaving men in the water. The Sunderland dropped a dinghy but returned to base damaged. Sunderland serial JM683 from the same squadron, flown by Flt. Lt. D.A. Sinclair, dropped another dinghy, but there were no survivors in the bitterly cold sea.
Ref: AIR 27/1914

This photograph was taken on 6 February 1944 with the nose camera of a Mosquito FBIV serial HP863 of 333 (Norwegian) Squadron, flown from Leuchars by Lt. Hans Engebrigtsen. The Mosquito crew was reconnoitring Bremangerfjord when they spotted a Heinkel He115B floatplane. After signalling to allay suspicion, Engebrigtsen got on to its tail and opened fire. The Heinkel returned fire but then burst into flames and crashed into the sea at Fröysjöen, killing the crew. It was on the strength of Küstenfliegerstaffel 1./406, a unit which operated with the German Navy.
Ref: AIR 15/472

On 14 February 1944, an experiment was carried out with night photography from a Wellington XII fitted with a Leigh Light. The test took place over the British submarine HMS *Umbra*, on which three bakelite bombs spaced at 80 ft were dropped from 40 ft while a 'Sea Search' photographic flash unit illuminated the target.
Ref: AIR 65/77

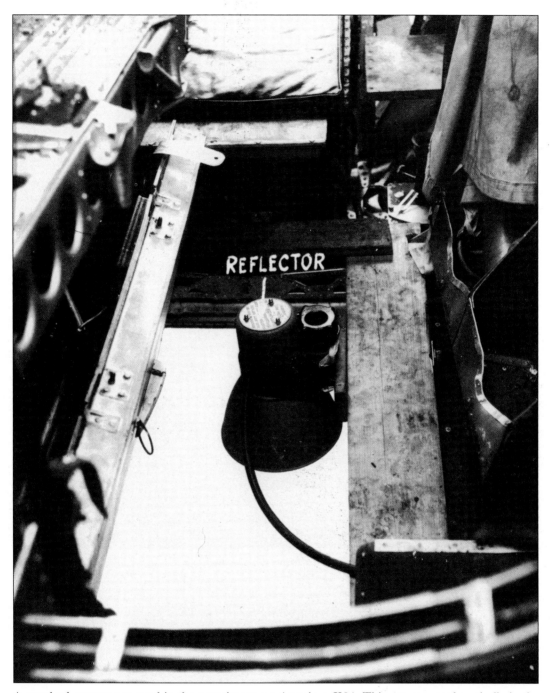

A standard camera was used in the experiment, an American K24. This was mounted vertically in the cockpit, with the photographs taken with the aid of a mirror. As with many such developments, the tests were carried out by the Coastal Command Development Unit, which initiated remarkable improvements in the efficiency of the anti-submarine and anti-shipping squadrons.
Ref: AIR 65/77

In the morning of 1 March 1944, three rocket-firing Beaufighters of 236 Squadron of the North Coates Strike Wing, supported by nine cannon-firing Beaufighters of 254 Squadron and nine of 143 Squadron, took off for an attack off Den Helder. The formation was led by Wg. Cdr. R.E. 'Paddy' Burns of 254 Squadron and escorted by Spitfires. They sighted a large merchant ship under tow by a tug, probably having struck a mine. She was escorted by about six flak ships, but the Beaufighters made a determined attack on all the vessels, scoring numerous hits. All the aircraft returned. Twenty-one Beaufighters of the Wing went out in the afternoon, again escorted by Spitfires, with three of 254 Squadron armed with torpedoes. They found the merchant vessel stationary and unescorted, and made another attack in which two torpedoes scored hits, as shown in this photograph. All the aircraft returned, but the German *Maasburg* of 6,415 tons was left on fire and soon sank.
Ref: AIR 28/595

The Leuchars Strike Wing, consisting of 455 (RAAF) and 489 (RNZAF) Squadrons, was officially formed in March 1944 with Beaufighter TFXs, although the two squadrons had been working in concert with these machines for several months. On 6 March 1944, four torpedo-carrying aircraft of 489 (RNZAF) Squadron with eight of 455 (RAAF) Squadron armed with cannon only, attacked a convoy of about sixteen ships off Stavanger, covered by German single-engined fighters. The Beaufighters scored numerous cannon hits, in spite of fire from the vessels and shore batteries. The German merchant vessel *Rabe* of 994 tons was sunk. Some of the Beaufighters avoided attacks from German fighters and all returned safely, with only one damaged.
Ref: AIR 28/471

On 7 March 1944, the North Coates Strike Wing was escorted by two squadrons of RAF Mustangs when it attacked a convoy of seven small ships, including three flak ships, near the German island of Borkum. Twenty-nine Beaufighters of 143, 236 and 254 Squadrons took part, with six of the latter carrying torpedoes. Although several vessels were set on fire by rockets and cannons, and two torpedoes were believed to have hit, there were no sinkings of enemy ships and two Beaufighters did not return. This photograph was taken from a Beaufighter of 254 Squadron.
Ref: 28/595

At 15.00 hours on 10 March 1944, Sunderland serial EK591 of 422 (RCAF) Squadron from Castle Archdale in Fermanagh was approaching a convoy about 450 miles west of the Shannon estuary when a U-boat was spotted. The flying boat was captained by Flt. Lt. S.W. Butler, with Warr. Off. F. Morton as 1st pilot. Butler dived, exchanging fire with the U-boat during which the Sunderland was hit, and dropped six depth charges across his target as it dived. It resurfaced shortly afterwards, moving at slow speed, and actually signalled visually to the Sunderland, congratulating the crew on bombing accuracy. The Sunderland remained over the U-boat until it finally sank by the stern at 17.40 hours, leaving men and dinghies in the water as shown in this photograph. Later identified as the Type VIIC *U-625* commanded by Oberleutnant zur See Siegfried Straub, it had left Brest on 29 February on a second war cruise. Unfortunately none of the U-boat men survived, although many took to their dinghies.
Ref: AIR 15/472

In the early afternoon of 23 March 1944, two Sunderlands of 461 (RAAF) Squadron from Pembroke Dock were attacked by enemy fighters while on patrol off the north-west of Spain. One Sunderland, serial ML740, captained by Plt. Off. F.J. Bunce, caught fire and was ditched in a heavy sea. Seven of the crew, including the captain, were able to get into the two dinghies, but the other five men were lost. At 09.10 hours on 25 March the dinghies were located about 150 miles north-west of El Ferrol in Spain by another Sunderland of 461 (RAAF) Squadron, captained by Flt. Lt. N.N. McKeough. An H-Type dinghy and other supplies were dropped. A Liberator of 547 Squadron, flown from St Eval by Fg. Off. J. King, arrived at 12.37 hours and dropped a Lindholme dinghy which was not recovered by the survivors. However, the destroyer HMS *Saladin* was guided to the spot and picked up the men at 15.00 hours, fifty hours after the ditching. Only one man was slightly injured and all seven survivors were landed at Mount Batten the following day.
Ref: AIR 27/1914

In the afternoon of 29 March 1944, the North Coates Strike Wing attacked a convoy north-east of Borkum. The force consisted of nine Beaufighters of 254 Squadron, six of which carried torpedoes, ten of 236 Squadron with rocket projectiles and cannons, and ten of 143 Squadron with cannons only. They were escorted by two squadrons of Mustangs. The enemy convoy comprised sixteen merchant vessels in two columns, escorted by three minesweepers and one heavily armed Sperrbrecher. The formation attacked from the seaward side and torpedoes sank two German merchant vessels, the *Hermann Schulte* of 1,305 tons and the *Cristel Vinnen* of 1,894 tons, while all enemy ships were raked with cannon fire and rockets. One Beaufighter failed to return. This photograph was taken from a Beaufighter of 143 Squadron, which was led on the occasion by Sqn. Ldr. J.G. Lingard.
Ref: AIR 28/595

In the afternoon of 14 May 1944, the Langham Strike Wing despatched twelve Beaufighters of 455 (RAAF) Squadron and twelve of 489 (RNZAF) Squadron to the Dutch island of Ameland, escorted by fighters. These squadrons had moved from Leuchars a month before. Six of the Beaufighters of 489 (RNZAF) Squadron carried torpedoes and the formation was led by Wg. Cdr. Jack N. Davenport of the Australian squadron. They attacked a convoy consisting of four merchant vessels and sixteen escort

vessels, against intense flak and in poor visibility. The enemy defences included balloons and flame-throwers. One Beaufighter of the New Zealand squadron was shot down and several other aircraft were damaged, but the Dutch merchant vessel *Vesta* of 1,854 tons was hit by a torpedo and sunk. The German minesweeper, *M.435* of 750 tons, was also sunk, either by a torpedo or cannon fire.
Ref: AIR 15/472

This remarkable photograph was taken early on 7 June 1944 from Sunderland III serial ML760 of 201 Squadron, flown from Pembroke Dock by Flt. Lt. L.H. Baveystock on a night patrol. The Sunderland was about 100 miles north of El Ferrol in Spain when a contact was picked up on radar. By coincidence, a Sunderland of 461 (RAAF) Squadron homed on the target at the same time as Baveystock and also dived on the target. Both aircraft dropped flares but no depth charges. Baveystock remained in the area and another radar contact was made almost three hours later, at 03.00 hours. He made a diving attack and the U-boat opened fire but was silenced by the Sunderland's guns. Six depth charges were dropped as well as flares, as shown in this photograph. The Type VIIC *U-955*, commanded by Oberleutnant zur See Hans Baden, was sunk with all hands. It was returning from its first war cruise, having left Bergen on 1 April.
Ref: AIR 15/472

On D-Day, 6 June 1944, three German destroyers left Royan in the Gironde estuary to harry the western flank of the Allied invasion force. These were the Narvik class *Z-32* commanded by Fregattenkapitän von Berger and *Z-24* commanded by Fregattenkapitän Heinz Birnbacher, together with the former Dutch *ZH-1* commanded by Korvettenkapitän Klaus Barckow. They were attacked in the afternoon by the Davidstow Strike Wing, comprising sixteen Beaufighters of 144 Squadron armed with cannons and fourteen of 404 (RCAF) Squadron armed with rockets and cannons. The formation was led by Wg. Cdr. David O.F. Lumsden of 144 Squadron and escorted by eight Mosquitos of 248 Squadron. Both *Z-32* and *Z-24* were seriously damaged and the destroyer flotilla put into Brest. One Beaufighter ditched on the return journey but the crew was picked up safely. The Germans put their dead and wounded ashore and patched up the destroyers. The German flotilla put to sea again on 8 June, together with the torpedo boat *T-24*, but was attacked near the Ile de Batz by the Allied 10th Destroyer Flotilla. *ZH-1* was sunk and *Z-32* was beached on the island while on fire, while the other two warships were beaten off. Escorted by Spitfires, the Davidstow Strike Wing finished off *Z-32* on 9 June, as shown in this photograph taken by a Boston of the RAF Film Unit which accompanied the force.
Ref: AIR 15/472

On D-Day, German Naval Forces sent fifteen U-boats from Brest to attack the western flank of the Allied invasion armada. Most of them were sunk by the RAF's Coastal Command or the Royal Navy. The U-boat in this photograph, the Type VIIC *U-821* commanded by Oberleutnant zur See Ulrich Knackfuss, was attacked at midday on 10 June 1944 by four Mosquito VIs of 248 Squadron from Portreath in Cornwall, armed with cannons and machine-guns. In the course of the attack, Liberator VI serial EV903 of 206 Squadron arrived on the scene, flown from St Eval by Flt. Lt. A.D.S. Dundas. The crew dropped five 250 lb depth charges on a first attack and six more on a second. The U-boat sank stern first, leaving a few survivors in the water while oil, debris and bubbles came to the surface.
Ref: AIR 37/1231

Coastal Command launched a large combined attack in the early morning of 15 June 1944 against a north-bound enemy convoy off the Dutch island of Schiermonnikoog, consisting of two large merchant vessels escorted by seven minesweepers. Nineteen Beaufighters of 236 and 254 Squadrons from the North Coates Strike Wing joined up with twenty-three of 455 (RAAF) and 489 (RNZAF) Squadrons from the Langham Strike Wing. They were escorted by a squadron of Mustangs and the formation was led by Wg. Cdr. Anthony Gadd, the 'Wing Commander Flying' at North Coates. The attack was completely successful. The German experimental *Schiff 49* of 7,900 tons (formerly the Dutch *Amerskerk*) and the Belgian merchant vessel *Gustav Nachtigall* of 3,500 tons were torpedoed and sunk. The minesweeper *M.103* of 772 tons was hit by rockets and blew up, while all the other minesweepers were damaged. All the aircraft returned, although some were damaged by flak.
Ref: AIR 15/472

Liberator III serial FL916 of 86 Squadron, flown by Flt. Lt. G.W.T. Parker, was on patrol from Tain in Ross-shire on 26 June 1944 when a U-boat was sighted at 23.30 hours about 100 miles north of the Shetlands. Two attacks were made, dropping three depth charges on each occasion. The first stick fell short but the second sank the U-boat. It was later identified as the Type VIIC *U-317*, commanded by Oberleutnant zur See Peter Rahlff, on its first war cruise from Egersund in Norway, and there were no survivors. The Liberator was hit by cannon fire but landed safely at Stornaway in the Hebrides, since Tain was closed in with bad weather.

Ref: AIR 15/472

By Opposing End Them

July 1944 – May 1945

With the Allied invasion force firmly established in Normandy by July 1944 and beginning to break out of its bridgehead, the squadrons of Coastal Command made strenuous efforts to help eliminate the Kriegsmarine in western France and deny the all-important U-boat bases in the Bay of Biscay to the enemy. The Strike Wings in Cornwall were reinforced with detachments drawn from the east of England. The Beaufighters and Mosquitos rampaged down the coast and sank ship after ship, including many naval vessels. By the end of August there were no targets left to attack and the squadrons began to move to the new bases of Strubby in Lincolnshire and Banff in Scotland. The North Coates Strike Wing remained in its old base for the remainder of the war, but the Langham Strike Wing moved north in October to Dallachy in Scotland. The German convoys along the coasts of Norway, Denmark, Germany and Holland received the full force of their enormous fire-power and suffered accordingly in some of the most violent attacks of the war.

The surviving U-boats left their bases in France and streamed round Ireland to Norway. In an effort to fight back against adversity, Grand Admiral Doenitz ordered U-boats fitted with Schnorkel tubes to concentrate on the waters round the British Isles, and these proved difficult to locate from the air, even though their approximate positions were known to British Intelligence. For this purpose, the 'Sonobuoy' was introduced into Coastal Command and several Liberator squadrons were equipped with it by the end of the year. The device consisted of a floating radio transmitter with a hydrophone which picked up the noise of a U-boat's propellers. When a pattern of several sonobuoys was dropped, the aircraft could locate the position of a submerged U-boat and a homing torpedo could be dropped. However, the problem of knowing where to drop the buoys was not fully mastered during the war, although Magnetic Anomaly Detector (MAD) equipment was being developed for use in aircraft. This identified the location of a submarine from the disturbance it caused in the earth's normal magnetic field.

One answer to the renewed threat of the U-boat, including the larger and faster versions which were coming into service as well as the new midget submarines, was to bomb the production centres where parts were made as well as the transport facilities which brought these to German shipyards for assembly. This task was mainly undertaken by Bomber Command and the US Eighth Air Force, but Coastal Command's Halifaxes joined in attacks against ports. Another measure was to destroy new U-boats when they left their training area in the Baltic and made their way to operational ports.

By the end of 1944, the strength of Coastal Command had increased to 1,081 aircraft, almost six times the number of the largely obsolete and unsuitable machines with which it had begun the war. The modern force included 128 Beaufighters, 70 Mosquitos, 219 Liberators, 28 Halifaxes, 88 Sunderlands and 119 Leigh

Light Wellingtons. Apart from these, there were 79 unarmed Spitfires and Mosquitos in the photo-reconnaissance squadrons, a mixed assortment of 128 in the meteorological squadrons and 70 aircraft in air-sea rescue. It was a formidable force, with highly trained crews, and it grew still further before the end of the war.

The advance of the Allies rendered Rotterdam useless to the Germans in autumn 1944 and thereafter the North Coates Strike Wing concentrated mainly on the German coast, Denmark and south-west Norway. It also sank a number of the midget submarines which were attempting to infiltrate British waters. The squadrons of the Strubby Strike Wing moved north to join the Dallachy Strike Wing in October, and enemy vessels in Norwegian waters became their targets for the remainder of the war. Before long, the Germans realized that it was impossible to move convoys during the day. The vessels sheltered in fjords, protected by shore batteries and flak ships, and sailed only at night. Of course, the Strike Wings sought them out in their

daytime anchorages and attacks took place in the fjords, resulting in numerous sinkings and, incidentally, some of the most dramatic action photographs of the war. They also sank several U-boats which were streaming out of the Baltic as the Russians advanced and heading to Norway.

When the war ended on 8 May 1945, Coastal Command was in complete ascendancy over the enemy. It had sunk forty-nine U-boats since the previous July and almost completed the destruction of the remaining surface vessels which were operating along enemy coasts. The inadequate force which began the war had grown to astonishing proportions, supported by British and American industry, a huge training scheme and remarkable scientific developments. It had fought a war against legitimate military targets and against a powerful, resourceful and courageous enemy, not without an element of chivalry on both sides. The remarkable achievements of Coastal Command in the war are, however, seldom recognized, even by some air historians.

This Type VIIC U-boat was attacked in the early afternoon of 8 July 1944 by Sunderland serial W4030 of 10 (RAAF) Squadron, flown from Mount Batten under the captaincy of Fg. Off. W.B. Tilley, when about 225 miles west of St Nazaire. It was *U-243*, commanded by Kapitänleutnant Hans Märtens, which had sailed from Bergen on 15 June to attack the western flank of the Allied invasion force. It was on the surface when Tilley dived and dropped six depth charges while his front gunner exchanged fire with the enemy, as shown in this photograph. The U-boat was obviously in extreme difficulties when Sunderland serial JM684 of 10 (RAAF) Squadron arrived, captained by Flt. Lt. R.E. Cargeeg, as well as a B-24 Liberator of the USNAF. Both dropped depth charges but these fell short and the U-boat sank from the first attack, while the crew launched dinghies. Tilley dropped another dinghy to the survivors and an Allied warship picked up thirty-nine men, but Märtens died of his wounds.
Ref: AIR 37/1231

On 8 July 1944, the North Coates Strike Wing combined with the Strubby Strike Wing to attack a convoy south-west of Heligoland. There were thirty-nine Beaufighters from 144, 254 and 236 Squadrons and 404 (RCAF) Squadron, led by Wg. Cdr. Anthony Gadd, who took over command of 144 Squadron shortly afterwards. The target consisted of six merchant vessels with ten escort vessels, which put up concentrated flak. Of these, the German merchant vessel *Tannhauser* of 3,200 tons, the Swedish *Sif* of 1,437 tons, the German *Miranda* of 736 tons, the German minesweeper *M.264* of 736 tons were sunk, as well as (by accident) the air-sea rescue launch *555* of 58 tons. Several aircraft were hit but all returned.
Ref: AIR 15/472

On 15 July 1944 the Langham Strike Wing ranged as far as Cape Lindesnes on the southern Norwegian coast. Wg. Cdr. Jack N. Davenport led thirty-four Beaufighters of 144 Squadron, 455 (RAAF) Squadron and 489 (RNZAF) Squadron against a tanker and four merchant vessels protected by five escort vessels. The Norwegian tanker *Irania* of 2,249 tons was badly damaged but managed to reach Oslo, and several other vessels were left on fire. All the Beaufighters returned safely.
Ref: AIR 15/472

The Davidstow Moor Strike Wing in Cornwall, consisting of 236 and 404 (RCAF) Squadrons, despatched twenty-four Beaufighters on an armed sweep down the west of France on 8 August 1944. Led by Wg. Cdr. A. Ken Gatward of 404 (RCAF) Squadron, they came across four M-class minesweepers in Bourgneuf Bay, near the mouth of the Loire, and attacked with rockets and cannons. One Beaufighter was shot down and its two crew members were killed, but the four minesweepers were sunk. They were *M.366*, *M.367*, *M.428* and *M.438*, all of 637 tons.
Ref: AIR 15/472

On 13 August 1944, Wg. Cdr. Anthony Gadd led ten Beaufighters of 236 Squadron and eight of 404 (RCAF) Squadron, part of the Davidstow Strike Wing, to the mouth of the Gironde on an anti-shipping sweep. They attacked the huge flak and mine destructor ships *Sperrbrecher 6* (formerly the *Magdeburg*) of 6,128 tons and *Sperrbrecher 5* (formerly the *Schwanheim*) of 5,339 tons with rockets and cannons. Both vessels were left burning and sinking, as shown in this photograph of *Sperrbrecher 6*. One Beaufighter and crew of 236 Squadron was lost.
Ref: AIR 15/472

In the late afternoon of 24 August 1944, the Davidstow Moor Strike Wing despatched ten Beaufighters of 236 Squadron and ten of 404 (RCAF) Squadron to Le Vernon in the Gironde estuary. The formation was led by Wg. Cdr. E.W. 'Bill' Tacon and their targets were the German destroyer *Z.24* of 2,603 tons and the torpedo boat *T.24* of 1,294 tons. They attacked with rockets and cannons against a hail of flak. *T.24* was holed below the waterline and sank almost immediately. *Z-24* capsized and sank later in the day. Miraculously, none of the Beaufighters was shot down, although fifteen were badly damaged. One ditched on the return journey and the men were picked up later. Five force-landed at Vannes airfield, which had been recently occupied by the Allies. This was the last major attack required of Coastal Command's anti-shipping squadrons in Cornwall. They were able to move north and concentrate on the Norwegian coastline.
Ref: AIR 37/1231

The Vickers Warwick was designed as a bomber but the performance of the prototype proved disappointing. Some of the first production run were converted to air-sea rescue duties with Coastal Command, carrying an airborne lifeboat as shown in this photograph of an aircraft of 281 Squadron. ASR Warwicks first entered squadron service in October 1943, and the crews carried out many rescues until the end of the war and beyond.
Ref: AIR 15/472

September 1944 was an extremely busy month for the air-sea rescue services, in which Coastal Command played a major part. A total of 251 sorties was made, and the service as a whole picked up 330 men, of whom 205 were glider or Dakota crews participating in the airborne assault on Arnhem. This photograph shows a ditched General Aircraft Hamilcar glider, which was used mainly to transport freight such as light tanks and ordnance to the landing zones.
Ref: AIR 15/472

The de Havilland Mosquito VI began to enter service with Coastal Command in December 1943, in both the fighter and bomber roles. Armed with four 20-mm cannons and four .303-in machine-guns, it could also carry 2,000 lb of bombs in the fuselage and under the wings, or eight rocket projectiles under the wings. Another version, the Mark XVIII known as the Tsetse, was fitted with a 57-mm anti-tank gun

instead of the cannons. The powerful and effective Mosquito played a major part in the Strike Wings which operated in 1944 and 1945, alongside the Beaufighter. This Mosquito of the Banff Strike Wing was photographed while returning to base with flak damage.
Ref: AIR 26/597

Twenty-one Beaufighters of 144 and 404 (RCAF) Squadrons from the Dallachy Strike Wing combined with seventeen Mosquitos of 235 and 248 Squadrons from the Banff Strike Wing in an attack on 15 October 1944. Twelve of the Beaufighters of 404 (RCAF) Squadron carried rockets. Led by Sqn. Ldr. W.R. Christison, they attacked the Norwegian tanker *Inger Johanne* of 1,202 tons and the flak ship *Vp1605* of 426 tons off Kristiansand, and sank both vessels without loss to themselves. The tanker disappeared amidst flame and smoke, as shown in this photograph, leaving burning oil and survivors in the water. Ref: AIR 26/597

On 23 October 1944, twenty-one Mosquitos of 235 and 248 Squadrons from the Banff Strike Wing, led
by Wg. Cdr. R.A. Atkinson of 235 Squadron, attacked several small ships in Hjeltefjord with bombs,
six-pounder shells and cannon fire. They sank the flak ship *V.5506 'Zick'* of 220 tons; she was the former
torpedo boat *Trygg* of the Norwegian Navy, which had been sunk in 1940 but later raised and repaired
by the Germans. The Norwegian merchant vessel *Biri* of 940 tons was also damaged in the attack. All
aircraft returned safely.
Ref: AIR 26/597

On 4 November 1944 the Banff Strike Wing despatched sixteen Mosquitos of 235 and 248 Squadrons, led by Wg. Cdr. G.D. 'Bill' Sise, to attack shipping in Florö harbour. They damaged a merchant vessel and a flak ship, which were left burning, but there are no German records of a sinking on this occasion. One Mosquito of 235 Squadron was shot down near the target.
Ref: AIR 26/597

On 8 November 1944, twenty-two Beaufighters of the Dallachy Wing made an attack against enemy ships in Midtgulenfjord. Led by Wg. Cdr. Anthony Gadd and guided by a single Mosquito of 333 (Norwegian) Squadron from Banff, they attacked a number of ships at anchor with rockets and cannons. The German merchant vessels *Aquila* of 3,495 tons and *Helga Ferdinand* of 2,500 tons were sunk. Unfortunately the civilian Norwegian ship *Framnes* of 307 tons, which was steaming through the fjord on her regular run, was caught up in the attack and badly damaged. Several Norwegians were killed and wounded in her. Five Beaufighters were hit by return fire but all returned to Dallachy.
Ref: AIR 15/472

The Banff Strike Wing despatched thirty-three Mosquitos of 143, 235 and 248 Squadrons, including one from the RAF Film Unit, to Nordgulenfjord on 5 December 1944. Led by Wg. Cdr. G.D. 'Bill' Sise, they came across two German convoys, one north-bound and the other south-bound, at anchorage under the shelter of steep cliffs near the village of Svelgen. There were four merchant ships, a tug and six flak ships. A wall of fire met the attackers but they dived down and fired cannons while some released rockets or fired six-pounder shells. They severely damaged the German merchant vessels *Ostland* of 5,273 tons, *Tucuman* of 4,621 tons, *Magdalena* of 3,283 tons and *Helene Russ* of 993 tons, although one Mosquito was shot down and several others were damaged. All these vessels were left in a shambles, on fire and with ammunition exploding, but they were so close to the shore that the Germans were able to prevent sinkings.
Ref: AIR 26/597

On 16 December 1944, the Frenchman Wg. Cdr. J.M. Maurice (whose real name was Max Guedj) led twenty-two Mosquitos of the Banff Strike Wing in an attack against shipping in the narrow Krakhellesund, just north of Sognefjord. The squadrons participating were Nos 143, 235 and 248, with an outrider from 333 (Norwegian) Squadron. They came across the German merchant vessel *Ferndale* of 5,684 tons, which had been part of a north-bound convoy the day before but had become stuck on rocks underwater. She was attended alongside by the salvage vessel *Parat*, while nearby under the cliffs were the flak ship *V.5305 'Flamingo'* and the tug *Fairplay X*. The Mosquitos attacked and set both *Ferndale* and *Parat* on fire, but one aircraft was hit and forced to ditch. An hour later, Wg. Cdr. G.D. 'Bill' Sise arrived at the head of six more Mosquitos and completed the destruction of both vessels, although one aircraft was hit and crashed into the side of a cliff, killing both men.
Ref: AIR 26/597

On 10 January 1945, Sqn. Ldr. W.R. Christison led the Dallachy Strike Wing, consisting of eight Beaufighters of 404 (RCAF) Squadron together with fourteen of 489 (RNZAF) and 455 (RAAF) Squadrons to the Norwegian coast. They were accompanied by two outrider Mosquitos of 333 (Norwegian) Squadron and two air-sea rescue Warwicks of 279 Squadron from Fraserburgh and escorted by ten Mustangs of 315 Squadron from Peterhead. They came across an anti-submarine vessel north of Lepsöy Island, near Ålesund, causing two explosions from their attack. An M-class minesweeper nearby was also left on fire. Two Beaufighters crashed during the attacks. There are no German records of sinkings at this time and place.

Ref: AIR 27/1786

The North Coates Strike Wing made a very courageous attack on 17 January 1945 when thirty-two Beaufighters were sent to the heavily defended anchorage of Marsdiep off Den Helder. They were armed with rockets and cannons and led by the commanding officer of 254 Squadron, Wg. Cdr. David L. Cartridge. Two squadrons of Spitfires escorted the formation. The main target was the hull of a *Hanso* ship of about 6,500 tons which had been built in Rotterdam under an emergency shipbuilding programme and was being sent to Germany for completion. It was protected by four minesweepers and four flak ships. The Beaufighters flew into intense flak from these as well as heavy fire from shore batteries. Four were shot down and two more collided, probably after being hit. Eleven others were damaged but managed to return home. They left the hull, two minesweepers and one flak ship in flames, but there were no sinkings. This was a black day for the North Coates Strike Wing, for nine of the twelve men who did not return were killed.
Ref: AIR 15/473

Fire in the starboard engine during an air test on 22 January 1945 at Banff resulted in the crash-landing of this Beaufighter of 404 (RCAF) Squadron flown by Fg. Off. J.R. Savard. The aircraft came down on

top of a hill at Fochabers, about 2 miles from the airfield, but fortunately Savard was not injured.
Ref: AIR 27/1786

The Banff Strike Wing despatched eighteen Mosquitos of 143, 235 and 248 Squadrons to Eidsfjord on 25 January 1945, led by Sqn. Ldr. H.H.K. Gunnis of 248 Squadron. They made a very effective attack with cannons and rockets on a stationary convoy of three merchant vessels accompanied by a flak ship and sank two of them, the German *Ilse Fritzen* of 5,099 tons and the Norwegian *Bjergfin* of 696 tons. Only one Mosquito was hit by return fire and all returned to Banff, but one was involved in a collision with another aircraft over the airfield and spun into the ground, the crew being killed.
Ref: AIR 26/597

The Banff Strike Wing made a devastating attack on 17 March 1945 when thirty-one Mosquitos of 143, 235 and 248 Squadrons, accompanied by two outriders of 333 (Norwegian) Squadron, attacked merchant ships at anchorage in Ålesund. They attacked with cannons and rockets, sinking the German *Iris* of 3,323 tons, the German *Remage* of 1,830 tons and the Norwegian *Log* of 1,684 tons. The German *Erna* of 865 tons was severely damaged. There was intense flak from the shore and two Mosquitos were shot down. One crashed in flames but the crew of the other got into their dinghy and were taken prisoner. The latter was flown by Wg. Cdr. Roy K. Orrock, the commanding officer of 248 Squadron, who led the formation.

Ref: AIR 26/597

Thirty-eight Mosquitos of the Banff Strike Wing took off for the Norwegian coast on 23 March 1945, together with three Mosquito outriders of 333 (Norwegian) Squadron and Mustang escorts. On arrival at the coast, the Mosquitos of 143, 235 and 248 Squadrons split away from one another and headed for three different fjords, each guided by an outrider. Twelve Mosquitos of 235 Squadron and one outrider, led by Sqn. Ldr. R. Reid, attacked the German merchant vessel *Rotenfels* of 7,854 tons in Dalsfjord, as shown in this photograph. She was protected by a flak ship, but was left on fire with many German dead. Sqn. Ldr. Reid's aircraft was hit and seen to dive into the sea near the target. His body was never found but that of his navigator was washed ashore. Their attack made such a deep impression on the local Norwegians that they erected a monument to their memory.
Ref: AIR 26/597.

Forty-one Mosquitos of the Banff Strike Wing, drawn from 143, 235 and 248 Squadrons together with two outriders of 333 (Norwegian) Squadron, took off on 2 April 1945 for Sandefjord. Led by the commanding officer of 248 Squadron, Wg. Cdr. H.N. Jackson-Smith, they attacked with cannons and rockets. Two merchant ships were sunk, the Norwegian *Concordia* of 5,154 tons and the German *William Blumer* of 3,604 tons. Two more were severely damaged, the German *Espana* of 7,465 tons and the German tanker *Kattegat* of 6,031 tons, while others were less seriously damaged. Two Mosquitos were hit, but they headed for sanctuary in Sweden instead of risking the return journey over the sea. Ref: AIR 26/597

The Banff Strike Wing was presented with the unusual opportunity of sinking U-boats in the afternoon of 9 April 1945. Thirty-five Mosquitos of 143, 235 and 248 Squadrons took off, as well as two outriders from 333 (Norwegian) Squadron and one from the RAF Film Unit. Led by Sqn. Ldr. H.H.K. Gunnis of 248 Squadron and escorted by Mustangs from Peterhead, they were over the Kattegat when the wakes of U-boats were spotted. These were the Type IX *U-804* commanded by Leutnant zur See Herbert Meyer and the Type VII *U-1065* commanded by Leutnant zur See Johann Panitz, on passage from Kiel to Horton in Norway. Both U-boats exploded from hits by cannons and rockets, but the explosion of *U-804* caught the Mosquito from the RAF Film Unit, which turned on its back and dived into the sea, killing the occupants. Three other Mosquitos were damaged but landed safely in Sweden. A Mosquito of 235 Squadron flown by Fg. Off. A.J. Randell, which had been escorting a Mosquito returning to Banff with engine trouble, then arrived on the scene after the main force had departed. This came across yet another U-boat, Type IX *U-843* commanded by Leutnant zur See Oscar Herwatz, which was a blockade runner returning from Djakarta and heading for Kiel. Randell made three attacks, scoring hits with rockets and sinking the U-boat. In the three U-boats, 144 German submariners were killed.
Ref: AIR 26/597

Wg. Cdr. A.H. 'Junior' Simmonds led thirty-five Mosquitos of 143, 235, 248 and 333 (Norwegian) Squadrons from the Banff Strike Wing on 11 April 1945 against merchant vessels at Porsgrunn. They sank the Norwegian *Dione* of 1,620 tons, the German *Kalmar* of 964 tons, the Norwegian *Nordsjo* of 178 tons and the Norwegian *Traust* of 190 tons. In additon, they left the German *Helgoland* of 535 tons and the Swedish *Skagen* of 219 tons severely damaged. Two Mosquitos were lost.
Ref: AIR 26/597

On 2 May 1945, Sqn. Ldr. A.G. Deck led thirty-five Mosquitos of 143, 235, 248, 333 (Norwegian) and 404 (RCAF) Squadrons from the Banff Strike Wing to the Kattegat. The Canadian squadron had converted to Mosquitos and transferred from the Dallachy Strike Wing in April. They sank the Type XXIII U-boat *U-2359*, which was en route to Norway under the command of Leutnant zur See G. Bischoff, and damaged another Type XXIII. The minesweeper *M.293* of 637 tons was also sunk. One damaged Mosquito headed for Sweden.
Ref: AIR 26/597

The last major operation of the Banff Strike Wing took place on 4 May 1945 when the commanding officer of 143 Squadron, Wg. Cdr. Christopher N. Foxley-Norris, led forty-three Mosquitos of 143, 235, 248 and 333 (Norwegian) Squadrons to the port of Aarhus on the west coast of Denmark, escorted by Mustangs. They sank the German merchant ship *Wolfgang L.M. Russ* of 3,750 tons and badly damaged the Danish *Angamos* of 3,540 tons and the German *Gunther Russ* of 998 tons. The vessels were protected by two ex-Dutch gunboats, a German minesweeper and a flak ship. Three Mosquitos were damaged and headed for the neutral sanctuary of Sweden instead of risking the return journey.
Ref: AIR 26/597

Admiral Karl Doenitz, who was appointed Chancellor of Germany after Hitler killed himself on 30 April 1945, broadcast a message at 15.14 hours on 4 May ordering all U-boats to surrender. In all, forty-five U-boats were in the Atlantic or British inshore waters. The British Admiralty arranged the main reception area at Loch Eriboll near Scapa, and the U-boats were ordered to surface and fly black flags as tokens of surrender. This U-boat was intercepted, fully surfaced and showing navigation lights, on the night of 10/11 May by Sunderland III serial ML759 of 422 (RCAF) Squadron, flown from Pembroke Dock by Flt. Lt. R.B. Duclos. It was then photographed in the early morning, about 180 miles west of Land's End, flying the German ensign and the black surrender flag.
Ref: AIR 27/1830

A Victory Flight was held on Wednesday 9 May 1945 over Plymouth by the Sunderlands of 10 (RAAF) Squadron.
Ref: AIR 27/153

APPENDIX A

SOME PRO SOURCES OF COASTAL COMMAND PHOTOGRAPHS 1939–1945

ADM 199/905 1940–1945. Reports of Proceedings of HM Ships.

AIR 2/1370 1935–1939. Stranraer General-Purpose Seaplane.

AIR 2/1511 1935–1936. Anson General-Purpose Service Trials.

AIR 2/2928 1938–1941. Sunderland Seaplane Flight & Ground Trials.

AIR 2/5151 1941–1943. Botha I Aircraft Official Flying Trials.

AIR 15/263 Attacks on Enemy Shipping, Claims Mar 1941 – Mar 1942.

AIR 15/264 Attacks on Enemy Shipping, Claims Apr – Jun 1942.

AIR 15/265 Attacks on Enemy Shipping, Claims Jul – Oct 1942.

AIR 15/270 Attacks on Enemy Shipping, Claims Nov 1941 – May 1943.

AIR 15/271 Attacks on Enemy Shipping, Claims Mar 1940 – Feb 1943.

AIR 15/470 Coastal Command Review, Jan 1942 – Apr 1943.

AIR 15/471 Coastal Command Review, May 1943 – Dec 1943.

AIR 15/472 Coastal Command Review, Jan – Dec 1944.

AIR 15/473 Coastal Command Review, Jan – Jun 1945.

AIR 15/560 1940–1941. Operational requirements Coastal Command aircraft Blenheim Mk IV.

AIR 16/933 Nov 1940 – Aug 1945. Air Fighting Development Unit Reports.

AIR 26/597 Banff Mosquito Strike Wing, Sep 1944 – May 1945.

AIR 27/149 10 (RAAF) Sqn, Jul 1939 – Dec 1940.

AIR 27/150 10 (RAAF) Sqn, Jan–Dec 1941.

AIR 27/151 10 (RAAF) Sqn, Jan–Dec 1942.

AIR 27/152 10 (RAAF) Sqn, Jan–Dec 1943.

AIR 27/153 10 (RAAF) Sqn, Jan 1944 – Jun 1945.

AIR 27/472 48 Sqn, Jan–Dec 1942.

AIR 27/509 53 Sqn, 3 July 1940 – 25 June 1945 (extracted to CN 5/13).

AIR 27/560 59 Sqn, Appendices, Jan 1940 – May 1946.

AIR 27/1187 202 Sqn Appendices, Sep 1939 – Jun 1941.

AIR 27/1211 204 Sqn Appendices, Sep 1939 – Jun 1941 (extracted to CN 5/14).

AIR 27/1225 206 Sqn Appendices, May–Oct 1944.

AIR 27/1226 206 Sqn Appendices, Jun 1944.

AIR 27/1227 206 Sqn Appendices, Jan–May 1945.

AIR 27/1228 206 Sqn Appendices, undated.

AIR 27/1297 209 Sqn Appendices, Oct 1937 – May 1945.

AIR 27/1346 217 Sqn Appendices, Jan 1940 – May 1945.

AIR 27/1370 221 Sqn Appendices, Jul–Aug 1945.

AIR 27/1413 228 Sqn, Jan–Dec 1940.

AIR 27/1414 228 Sqn, Jan–Dec 1941.

AIR 27/1438 233 Sqn Appendices, Sep 1939 – Jun 1941.

AIR 27/1497 248 Sqn, Jan–Jun 1945.

AIR 27/1568 269 Sqn Appendices, Jan 1916 – Oct 1945.

AIR 27/1569 269 Sqn Appendices, May 1941 – Jun 1945.

AIR 27/1786 404 (RCAF) Sqn, 1 May 1941 – 25 May 1945.

AIR 27/1830 422 (RCAF) Sqn, 2 Apr 1942 – 5 Jun 1945.

AIR 27/1833 423 (RCAF) Sqn Appendices, Aug 1942 – Feb 1945.

AIR 27/1897 455 (RAAF) Sqn, Jun 1941 – Dec 1943.

AIR 27/1913 461 (RAAF) Sqn, Jan–Dec 1943.

AIR 27/1914 461 (RAAF) Sqn, Jan 1944 – May 1945.

AIR 27/1993 520 Sqn Appendices, May 1946.

AIR 28/48 Ballykelly Appendices, Dec 1945.

AIR 28/75 Bircham Newton Appendices, Dec 1939 – Dec 1940.

AIR 28/76 Bircham Newton Appendices, Jan–Nov 1941.

AIR 28/77 Bircham Newton Appendices, Dec 1941 – Jan 1943.

AIR 28/135 Castle Archdale Appendices, Dec 1944.

AIR 28/470 Leuchars Appendices, Oct 1939 – May 1940.

AIR 28/471 Leuchars Appendices, Jan 1940 – Jan 1944.

AIR 28/595 North Coates Appendices, Nov 1940 – Mar 1944.

AIR 28/631 Pembroke Dock, Dec 1939 – Oct 1944.

AIR 28/733 St Eval Appendices, Jan 1940 – Nov 1942.

AIR 28/741 St Eval Appendices, Jan 1943 – Aug 1944.

AIR 28/828 Thornaby Appendices, Sep 1939 – Oct 1943.

AIR 28/941 Wick Appendices, Dec 1939 – Mar 1940.

AIR 28/942 Wick Appendices, Apr 1940 – Aug 1941.

AIR 28/943 Wick Appendices, Sep 1941 – Mar 1942.

AIR 28/944 Wick Appendices, Jan 1943 – Jul 1944.

AIR 29/676 32 Operational Training Unit, Jul 1941 – May 1944.

AIR 37/1231 SHAEF photographic record of Allied air effort in support of invasion of Continent.

AIR 41/74 The RAF in Maritime War, Volume V. The Atlantic and Home Waters, Jun 1944 – May 1945.

AIR 65/77 14 Feb 1944. Photography of night low-level attacks with the Sea Search Photographic Unit, Type D-1, also known as the Edgerton Flash Unit.

AIR 65/84 7 Mar 1944. Illumination for night attacks on U-boats. Details Launcher Mk V and 1.7 in flares.

AIR 65/94 15 Apr 1944. Illumination of low-level night attacks on U-boats (first report).

AIR 65/100 15 May 1944. Ciné photography of low-level attacks.

AIR 65/109 2 Jul 1944. Automatic photography of low-level night attacks with $1\frac{1}{2}$ in photo-flash cartridges in Leigh Light Wellington aircraft.

AIR 65/112 5 Jul 1944. Night rocket projectile attacks on submarine with the aid of Leigh Light and MK III Air to Surface-Vessel.

AIR 65/121 29 Jul 1944. Performance of Pumpkin searchlight Type B in Halifax GR aircraft.

AIR 65/131 2 Sep 1944. Automatic photography at night using $1\frac{1}{2}$ in photo-flash cartridge.

AIR 65/166 27 Feb 1945. Automatic photography of low-level night attacks with $1\frac{1}{2}$ in cartridge.

AVIA 7/1493 1942. ASV Installation in Whitley aircraft.

AVIA 16/10 1935. Torpedo release mechanism on Vildebeest aircraft.

AVIA 16/27 1938. Trial of air rudders on Vildebeest aircraft.

AVIA 16/59 1941. 18-in torpedo trials on Catalina II aircraft.

AVIA 16/62 1942. 18-in torpedo trials on Hampden I aircraft.

AVIA 16/63 1942. 18-in torpedo trials on Wellington IC aircraft.

AVIA 16/67 1942. 18-in torpedo trials on Beaufighter VI aircraft.

AVIA 16/72 1942. The use of dive brakes in a Beaufort II aircraft.

AVIA 16/88 1943. Mark XII torpedoes fitted to Beaufighter, Beaufort & Hampden aircraft.

CN 1/5 1943–4. Extracted from ADM 1/12528. Flight paths of American Mk 24 mine and close-up of torpedo.

CN 1/39 Extracted from ADM 199/1422. Attacks by sea and air on U-boats in the North Atlantic.

CN 5/13 Extracted from AIR 27/509, 53 Sqn.

CN 5/14 Extracted from AIR 27/1211, 204 Sqn.

SUPP 9/1 Aircraft: Data Sheets and Photographs (British).

SUPP 9/2 Aircraft: Data Sheets and Photographs (American).

INDEX